THE BOOK GROUP BOOK

A Thoughtful Guide to Forming and Enjoying a Stimulating Book Discussion Group

ELLEN SLEZAK

CHICAGO REVIEW PRESS

Library of Congress Cataloging-in-Publication Data

The Book group book : a thoughtful guide to forming and enjoying a stimulating book discussion group / [edited by] Ellen Slezak.
    p.   cm.
  Includes bibliographical references.
  ISBN 1-55652-195-2 (pbk.) : $9.95
  1. Group reading—United States. I. Slezak, Ellen.
LC6651.B66 1993   93-25224
374'.22—dc20   CIP

Published by Chicago Review Press, Incorporated
814 North Franklin Street
Chicago, Illinois 60610

ISBN 1-55652-195-2

Printed in the United States of America

5 4

CONTENTS

INTRODUCTION

I was in the thick of this project—visiting book groups, reading stacks of essays, typing thousands of book titles—when a friend called and invited me to join a book group that she had recently formed.

No way was I in the mood to make a book group commitment. Then she mentioned that her group was reading Isabel Allende's *The House of the Spirits* for its next meeting. I hesitated. That's one of those books on my why-haven't-I-made-time-to-read-that-yet list, especially after hearing so much about it from readers and writers across the country while working on this book. But then I looked again at the stack of manuscripts on my desk and the calendar hanging above it, thanked her for the invitation, and asked her to try me again next year.

Her call brought to light one of my favorite parts of this project—the discovery of new titles and the reexamination of books I already knew. As I selected and edited the essays and lists that constitute this book, I found myself searching my bookshelves for a certain title that someone had written about glowingly, wanting to remember how much I had liked it when I first read it. On the flip side, when I'd read somebody's statement that *The Mill on the Floss* was a flop, I'd bristle and mutter. And, of course, plenty of books that were high on somebody else's list had left me cold when I first read them— maybe I'd give them another shot.

From the essays I've read and the groups I've visited, it's clear that "giving it another shot" is one thing that book groups are all about. Many of the readers whose essays are included in this book write about the magic they feel during a meeting when the collective thought bubble hovering over the bowl of M&Ms and cups of herbal tea seems to read, "You know, I never thought about it that way." Or, as one book group leader shouted during a particularly heated discussion I witnessed, "Did we all read the same book?"

If I were a sociologist, I would do a study of book groups to answer that question and these others that come to mind: What is it that drives people to meet and talk about reading, a distinctly solitary endeavor? Why is it mostly women who do this? Of course, if I were a sociologist my list of questions would be much longer, but these two should do just fine for now. The book group members I met spoke of their monthly meetings as an oasis, a retreat, a salvation, something nurturing and binding. Most people were fierce in their loyalty to their book group, and those who felt this loyalty waning after being in a group for years felt plenty guilty about that. These groups fulfill different dreams and obligations for different people. They allow parents of young children a scheduled escape. They give those caught up in a demanding job a chance to relax. They offer tuition-free intellectual stimulation for others. As one committed book group member told me, "It was either this or grad school, and I think this has worked out better."

Another woman mentioned that before joining her book group it had taken her three years to finish *Lonesome Dove*—she'd carried it with her everywhere. Since joining a group, she'd read three books in three months and she'd gone into a bookstore just the other day and bought three books that weren't even on her group's reading list. Oh yeah, that's another reason people join book groups—book groups remind them that they like to read.

I struggled with the men question from the start. Most of the groups I visited were composed of women only—some by accident, many by design. An overwhelming majority of the essays I received were written by women about their all-women groups. I suspected there were plenty of men involved in book groups, but I hadn't run into many, and what about all the anecdotal evidence I'd found? It screamed that men just don't get it when it comes to book groups either. Being an accomplished fence straddler, I found myself unable to decide whether to ignore the issue or throw a spotlight on it.

Fortunately, the two male essay contributors to this book, Curt Matthews and Rodd Zolkos, shed some light. Matthews offers convincing evidence that men can be valuable members of a book group. He shows how the "intellectual equality" that his group fosters is one key to a successful marriage. His essay gives me hope that gender, when it comes to book groups and reading at least, doesn't matter. Well, Zolkos brought me down to earth with a thump and a laugh. His basic premise is that Book Group just isn't a tongue men can speak. Still, I think you'll find that the information in this book works equally well for women or men who want to start or join a group.

Plenty of bookstores and newsletters and libraries are willing to help. If you'd like to join a group, but don't know how to do it, start by talking to your local bookseller or librarian. I've learned about book groups that are run by professional leaders (that is, members pay a fee to belong to them), sponsored by independent or chain bookstores, and organized by public libraries. You'll read about some of these in this book.

Would-be or current book group members will also find a number of publications devoted to their needs. *BookLovers*, a bimonthly magazine (P.O. Box 93485, Milwaukee, WI 53203), focuses on book discussion groups, profiling a group in each issue, including lists of books that groups are reading, and publishing articles and reviews that help keep readers current on what's going on in the literary world. *Reading Women: The Newsletter of Literary Ideas*, also bimonthly (P.O. Box 296, Winnetka, IL 60093), offers in-depth reviews of titles, with an eye to works that lend themselves to book group discussion. The Hungry Mind bookstore publishes *Fodder: News from the Mind* (1648 Grand Ave., St. Paul, MN 55105), which among other things lists books that groups are reading and sometimes profiles a particular group.

The makeup and organization of the groups I visited varied greatly. The largest group I met was sponsored by a public library. It was led by a librarian who offered a plan, an outline, questions, comments, and coffee with powdered cream. She worked skillfully to draw members into the discussion. The group met to discuss Jill McCorkle's *Ferris Beach*. That morning the group was sixteen women and one man (an unusually small turnout, the librarian told me). They were mostly older—one woman joked that they should all be members of the "Senile Center." The leader kept things on track as members arced off to share stories about their lives. The discussion was lively. People laughed and joined in freely. The leader found the relevance in most comments or, when necessary, deftly steered the discussion back to the book. The meeting lasted about an hour.

This contrasts sharply with the very last group I visited—four women who have been meeting for a little more than a year. Initially, they tried to find others to join them, but a while ago they realized with guilty pleasure, one member confessed, that they liked the intimacy of their group. They've since stopped all efforts to expand. They meet every four to six weeks. They usually read on a theme (I was there for the last in a series of books about voodoo). Since they all enjoy cooking, they prepare careful, delicious dinners for each other (I was also there for grilled red snapper and Caribbean-style cabbage and red pepper salad). Their discussion of the book was interspersed with catching up on each others' jobs and personal lives. It meandered comfortably around food preparation, candle lighting, and strong coffee with dessert.

Everything happened naturally the night I visited this group. The book discussion was *the* reason for meeting, but ultimately it was only a part, fitting in with the wine and the food and the conversation to create the perfect atmosphere for developing friendships while learning something new.

For if reading is a solitary escape, a book group is a variation on the theme—that same escape with others. In the essay section of this book, you'll find groups that meet in the city, providing refuge for their members—an antidote for hectic jobs, traffic, and crowds. And then you'll read about groups in rural areas or small towns, where again the members see the group as a refuge, though this time from the solitude and remoteness that geography has placed upon them. It seems book groups are a refuge people approach from different directions.

I didn't know what to expect when I reached out in all those directions for essays, but apparently book group members are some of the most enthusiastic, generous, literate people around. Lots of them wanted to share the good fortune they feel in being part of a group. Putting out the call for essays was easy, narrowing it down to the thirty pieces you'll find in this book was much more difficult. I got caught up in each writer's enthusiasm—everybody *must* know about this group in Bemidji and that one in Brooklyn, and then I'd remind myself sternly that I had to make a choice.

I've tried to give a representative sampling of groups across the country. I found the contrasts most interesting, and many of my choices hinged on those. The story of the small newly established city group compared to the ladies' arts club that's been meeting for seventy-six years. The group with a strict rule about finishing the book next to the one whose members keep their fingers crossed in hope that somebody made it to the end. The story of the poetry reading group next to the poem from a member of a group that primarily reads works by African-American women. The saga of the group that broke up next to that of a group that managed to turn itself around as it was foundering. And a few writers tell us about an individual within their group who made a deep impression and really defined the group for them.

Book group members were equally generous in sharing their reading lists, which follow the essay section of this book. Many of the lists are arranged according to when the group read particular titles. I guess I would have to be a historian to ask the right questions about this section. What does it mean that groups were reading *The Feminine Mystique* in 1963, *The Women's Room* in 1978, and *Iron John*, *Backlash*, and *Sexual Personae* in 1992? In any case, the reading lists are testimony to how open-minded and curious book group members can be— *Iacocca* even shows up twice.

As I worked on the book list section, I often thought about the titles that would appear on future lists. As I write this, Dorothy Allison's *Bastard Out of Carolina* is just out in paperback, and I realize I have a new book-related affliction. My response to any book I read or read about is now, "hmmm, would that be a good book group book? . . ." I'll lay odds that Allison's novel will soon be on schedule for scores of groups across the country. And next year Robert Boswell's *Mystery Ride*, and the year after that Kaye Gibbons's *Charms for the Easy Life* and Barbara Kingsolver's *Pigs in Heaven*, and then. . . .

These titles will take root on book group lists naturally, reviews of them spreading by word of mouth—booksellers and librarians and readers relaying the news. And if a book group member goes into a bookstore to buy one of these books and forgets the title, she or he needn't worry. As one woman told me about her attempt to buy Terry McMillan's *Waiting to Exhale*, "I told the clerk I didn't know its name, but it was a popular book about four black women who go on vacation and it has something to do with inhaling." She walked out with the right book, part of the bookseller's job being to help untangle book group members who get their plot wires crossed.

In the last essay in this book, Lenore Baeli Wang writes about reading as her sustenance as a writer—about the change and action reading produces within her. She tells us that reading is her only hope as a writer. I look at that statement and at all the other essays in this book and think of how reading serves as a bridge to so many different places. Wang reads to sustain her writing, another reader uses reading to get closer to her daughter, someone else follows it as a blueprint for keeping a marriage strong.

Readers and writers. Book groups serve as a connection between the two. A direct route that's spotted with options— detours marked by the quirks and rules and people that make each book group distinctly different from any other. My friend who just started her group has many choices before her, but, as the writers in this book testify, whichever way she goes, she's in for a good ride.

PART I
Essays

Anybody who wants to start or join a Book Group should find plenty of useful, practical advice in the essays that make up this section. I hope that those who already are members of book groups will also gain something as they compare their group dynamics, structure, and rules with those of the groups described here. And every *reader*, book group member or not, will appreciate these glimpses of book group life, which prove that careful readers are an important part of every writer's work.

If you find a group that particularly interests you, you may be able to get an even more complete picture of it by checking the book lists in part II, since many of the essay contributors also shared reading lists.

ONCE BEGUN, WE ARE MIGHTY

Carol Huber
Morton, Washington

My book club has saved my life. We meet once a month to discuss a book we agreed to read. Sometimes we don't all read it, and sometimes we don't read it all, and some of us, I suspect, don't read it at all until it has been discussed by the club. This is a better way than most to choose reading material.

We live in and around Morton, Washington, where the hottest spot in town is Spiffy's Fine Dining and Car Wash, and it closes at six. The whole town closes at six. We have two groceries, one drugstore, a Boot Barn, and a Logger's Supply Store. But mostly what we have is trees. The nearest movie is an hour west, and the high school wag with the spray can has adjusted a Tacoma signpost to read "Taco 54 miles." This may be true; we have no fast food. So close to Mt. Rainier and Mt. St. Helens, we are allowed to eat bacon and eggs—it's not cholesterol that clogs our veins.

We are all women in our club, though Bert, the husband of one of the members, usually reads the book and sometimes hangs around for the discussion. Reading is women's work in this part of the woods.

Most of us are schoolteachers, two are wives of schoolteachers, one is a social service case worker, and one is a half-blind novelist. She reads talking books, and the rest of us get ours from the library in Randle. (We know, they spell it wrong.) Morton doesn't have a library. There was talk once of getting one. "What for?" people asked. "Who would use it?" There are 1,200 people here. Those who insist on reading drive to Randle.

Barb (Bert's wife), calls the librarian with our book list and those who have library cards get a copy in the mail. Those who don't, borrow and search out paperbacks or make the drive to Portland where there is a five-story bookstore. Obviously, they are servicing most of the Northwest. The novelist calls the man at Talking Books, and he sends tapes.

We read one book a month. We try not to choose really thick books two months in a row—it's hard for the schoolteachers to get their reading done. Still, the books on our list are frequently thick. Once a year we read a nonfiction book and a classic novel. Although only one person wanted to read *Tess of the d'Urbervilles*, she forced it on the group. She was the only one who finished the book—it was summer, and in summer we get feisty—and she visibly gloated. We have decided behind her back that she will not be allowed to choose another book. Our other rule is to avoid books being made into movies. This rule was passed after we read *Prince of Tides*, *Fried Green Tomatoes at the Whistle Stop Cafe*, and *Cold Sassy Tree*. We were very upset to discover in mid-book that *Paris Trout* was available on video.

We take turns leading the discussion and being the hostess. Our meetings go like this: about four of us are on time. Any four. These four usually know who is on the way, and who is not. Then we wait for Kathy. While we wait, we try not to talk about the book. Sometimes we spend this time deciding whose house we will visit and which books we will read. We keep about six months ahead. The novelist keeps insisting that while we may read *The Firm*, there will be nothing to discuss afterward.

When Kathy arrives, Barb steers us quickly into the discussion. Barb is our leader, though we give her no credit. We have to establish the book discussion quickly at this point for there is danger that the teachers will get going on some school stuff and the rest of us will not be able to stop them. They are much better since one of us asked pointedly one night if we were going to talk about the book at all.

There is a slow start. Nobody wants to commit herself. Here the danger lies. This is where it becomes likely that someone who has not finished the book will excuse herself by stating that she found the work difficult to "get into." At this point all nonfinishers quickly repeat the comment and the book is condemned. This is what happened to *Tess*.

When a real finisher jumps in with a comment, we are off. Even those who didn't get past the first chapter, and Janet, who had been in the bathroom finishing the last, are eager to share observations and delights. We almost had to carry discussion of *The River Why* over for a second month so some could finish. Once begun, we are mighty. It is not just because we love books. We know that whatever our family and career provides, this is our cultural hub. Recently I heard a musician say she couldn't take it in the woods. I guess you don't form a group to read sheet music.

There are about ten in our group when no one is gone to a soccer game or school board meeting. In winter, we can afford to miss a meeting. School is in and there may be black ice on the road. We start on time and break for home as soon as we are slaked. In summer, we lounge through a well-attended picnic meeting, and when Barb and Bert had cousins in from Holland we had a barbecue. Food and drink sessions last longer. New members are always welcome and are brought along by old members. We are friends in the truest sense, as dependent on each other as the Donner party. Where we live, our book group is life support.

HOW WE GOT TO BE SIX—AND WHY IT FEELS LIKE FORTY

Ann Christophersen
Chicago, Illinois

Next month my women's book group will celebrate its sixth anniversary. To mark the event, perhaps we'll read historian Gerda Lerner's new book, *The Creation of Feminist Consciousness*. There would be some symmetry in that, since the first book we took up was Lerner's *The Creation of Patriarchy*. Or maybe we'll wait until March since that's women's history month—Lerner will be in Chicago then to talk about the book at our feminist bookstore, Women & Children First, of which I'm co-owner. We could make it a group outing, have dinner afterward. On the other hand, we had already tentatively decided to read Marjorie Agosin's *Secret Weavers: Stories of the Fantastic by Women of Argentina and Chile*. That, too, is appropriate for that particular month, especially since we decided to make a conscious attempt to push our cultural boundaries (we are seven white women) and read more globally.

This is the monologue version of what we'll talk about collectively when we meet on Sunday to discuss Laura Esquivel's charming novel about food and life, *Like Water for Chocolate*, and plan for upcoming meetings.

Discuss, plan. And, oh yes, celebrate a recent birthday (I'll bring the angel food cake, a tradition), perform a house-blessing ritual, hear about a recent trip to Memphis (we've already heard she did see Elvis and wishes she hadn't), catch up on other news, and share a meal.

Our group has a name, the acronym WRAGE, but the translation of it, like a secret handshake or password, shall remain private. I'll give this clue: besides reflecting the feminist politics that are a crucial component of our identity, it underscores the gastronomic angle of our pursuits, which, indeed, rivals our intellectual and social raison d'être.

That's a slight exaggeration, for though we do love to eat and do hold dear the opportunity to keep track of important events in each others' lives, our main purpose is to talk about what we have spent hours reading and thinking about in the solitude of our homes and minds.

A simple statement, that. But it hasn't always been simple to translate privately held, often amorphous, material into coherent thoughts and statements. It hasn't always been easy to negotiate the rocky terrain of egos and personalities and the tensions that develop between people, even when those people like, respect, and care about each other. And it is difficult to learn how to talk intelligently about challenging works of fiction and nonfiction when there is no one in charge, no one designated to ask great questions, pursue and develop ideas, keep the group on track, and function as "the teacher."

And how do you manage to choose from the almost infinite list of books to find books that most of the group members will feel passionate about, or at least motivated to read and discuss? Since the very life of the group, not to mention the quality of its interactions, depends on the successful resolution of these challenges, a few more words on how our group has dealt with them might serve others struggling to build a thriving, stimulating group.

Determining what to read seems a logical place to start. When we first got together, we chose randomly. We had established two guidelines—that we wanted to read books by women and that if someone proposed a book any member of the group really didn't want to read, that member could nix it—beyond these rules, it was an open field. Because two of us worked in a bookstore and saw daily the newest offerings, and because several of us were avid readers of reviews as well as books, we tended to select titles just published. No one was averse to buying hardcover books, so we were able to satisfy our cravings and dive right into a tantalizing new novel or work of feminist theory or history without waiting for the paperback version to appear.

We hadn't established a system for actually settling on titles, though, and some of us were more forthcoming with suggestions than others. Soon, we'd slipped into the habit of shaking our heads in agreement while two or three people recommended what to read. This, of course, bred a certain passivity and lack of investment in the head-shakers and a corresponding presumption in the more aggressive members. They knew the others would most likely give the nod to their suggestions, even when those suggestions weren't particularly thoughtful. Being the more active member also carried some psychological risk, since a thumbs-down response could be interpreted as connoting questionable judgment, a worry the quieter members were able to avoid.

We remedied this for a time by devising a plan whereby everyone had equal input and responsibility for the process. Periodically, we would devote part of a monthly meeting to choosing books for the next seven months (the number of members in the group). Each of us submitted a list of three titles and explained our interest in them. Then we voted on the one book in each person's set that we most wanted to read. The high votes became our list. This democratized the process, getting everyone involved and providing a way to make equitable *and* informed choices.

But it felt too formal and cumbersome and, probably more important, it locked us in. We value the freedom to read a new book *now*.

Our solution was to take time out every now and then and check in with each other to see how we feel about the list. Does anyone want to be reading more short fiction? More nonfiction? More books by Native women? Poetry? We are mature enough now—seasoned, crusty, self-aware, and trusting—to speak up. Getting to this point is the natural outcome and reward for staying together, experimenting, and struggling in a conscious way to accommodate each others' and the group's best interest.

Choosing good books is, I think, the preeminent work of a discussion group. If you choose well, even when you don't have a brilliant discussion, at least you have the satisfaction of reading something you might otherwise have missed. But if you can also manage to talk about that good book, to coax out the ideas, images, allusions, and language—meaning that may have escaped you in its fullness before the discussion—then you have wrought gold from iron.

There have been many such moments in my group, but one of the most memorable for me came while talking about Sandra Cisneros's wonderful collection of stories, *Woman Hollering Creek*. Cisneros employs an extraordinary range of voices, from a young girl in "Eleven" to the Mexican revolutionary's patient lover in "Eyes of Zapata." We had selected a few stories to focus on (a useful device we've discovered to help shape a coherent discussion when reading a volume of short or disparate pieces), and one of these, "Remember the Alamo," was puzzling. Who, exactly, is the narrator? We talked and argued and said, "Yes, but what about. . . ." and after a while we came collectively to an understanding of this character that no one individually had before.

I don't know how to describe the elation I felt, but I can say that the process and the epiphany were equally thrilling. To me, it is why one engages with a group of people in an enterprise like this—to get somewhere intellectually that you can't get to by yourself.

We were able to accomplish this alchemy—transforming our raw, untempered thoughts into a finer material—because we were prepared to do it. That is, we had read the book carefully, reread and studied the central stories, marked key passages and images, taken note of the language, found the patterns, and raised some questions.

These are invariably the ingredients of a good meeting. In an attempt to leave it less to chance, we have taken lately to structuring our discussions somewhat. We've moved from having no leader and hoping that someone or everyone would raise questions and direct our talk, to having a single group leader who assumed that role, rotating the responsibility from month to month.

This has worked, but has some pitfalls—some people are more skillful than others, having more training, experience, or chutzpah, or, in spite of good intentions, the appointed leader may have a bad month at work or at home and arrive at our meeting disappointingly prepared.

Currently, the happy solution is to pair up. Two people share the load for each meeting. It's working beautifully so far. The two-heads-are-better-than-one rule is holding true, the twosomes are having a nice time during their interim get-together, and creativity and quality are at an all-time high.

Other ways we have struck on to raise the level and enjoyment of our conversations is to do secondary reading. People bring clippings of interviews with the author from *Publishers Weekly* or reviews from the *New York Times Book Review* or the *Women's Review of Books*. We're discussing *Jane Eyre* soon and someone has already pointed out that Adrienne Rich has a great essay on the subject in *On Lies, Secrets, and Silences*. When we read Jane Smiley's brilliant novel, *A Thousand Acres*, some of us read or reread *King Lear* or watched a production of it on video so we could better see how she used that tragedy in composing her own.

A word of warning here. It does not follow that careful preparation ensures the luxury of a smooth, congenial meeting. In our group, there are a number of books we have all loved, a number more that we have liked but struggled through (either in reading or discussing), and another batch that has brought forth conflicting views from different members. One of my favorite novels, the bizarre, funny, touching, minimalist *Mrs. Caliban* by Rachel Ingalls, met with little enthusiasm by at least half the group and outright antagonism by a few others. Most of us thought Toni Morrison's *Beloved* was one of the most profound novels we had ever read, while one member wasn't convinced by the supernatural rendering of the character Beloved. A few of us thought Anne Tyler's *Breathing Lessons* benign entertainment, while one of us gagged at its patriarchal stereotypes and to this day does not take kindly to suggestions of reading another Tyler novel. (I secretly read them all.) Some of us found Doris Lessing's *Fifth Child* a powerful, moving allegory, others, reductively simple and ghoulish.

Sometimes one has to set her teeth against the disappointment of not having her judgment and pleasure shared. But the truth is that some of the most interesting discussions we have had have been those in which there were wide-ranging opinions. At those meetings we often left vowing to give this novel another, perhaps more enlightened, reading, and that one a boot right out of our library. Or we think about endings more carefully. Or what good dialogue is and isn't.

Other times it's December and we don't have time to read and prepare three hundred pages. So we get together for a wonderful Italian soup, bread, salad, and red wine dinner and bring a page or paragraph from one of our favorite books to read aloud. Or it's the middle of summer and we are lazy, so we go to Michigan for a day and have a picnic and do a reading of Claudia Allen's play *Movie Queens*. Or we go to the movies and see *Strangers in Good Company* and leave vowing to take a trip together and to be as inspired when we are old women as the spirited women in that movie are.

And though we have always been friends, we haven't always gotten along. While actively solving intellectual and logistical problems has been half the pleasure and challenge over the years, resolving psychological and interpersonal ones has been the other. Early on, we often weren't very brave, retreating into the relative safety of self-effacement or understatement rather than risk a bold, clear opinion. Other times, in contrast, we were rash and insensitive, rushing to make our own point rather than elaborate on and extend the idea someone had already placed on the table. Tensions have developed inside and out of group meetings, leaving feelings frayed and requiring time and attention to restore full trust and comfort.

So we are six years old with a bit of gray at the temples, having earned a degree of maturity beyond our youthful age. But, of course, six years in the lives of conscious and committed women who speak the same political language and share similar emotional and intellectual goals is plenty of time to mold the monthly experience of reading together, talking together, and being together into a deeply satisfying shape. My thanks to Alice, Beth, Jean, Sally, Sara, and Susan for making it so.

THE MODERN LITERATURE CLUB

Ellen Shipley and Kim Harington
Fayetteville, Arkansas

The love of books can be a powerful bond. The Modern Literature Club of Fayetteville, Arkansas, is one of the oldest women's clubs in the area. Seeking good literature and then reviewing and discussing its pleasures and profundities has unified these women in a compelling way. This union and the desire to sustain its rewards is so strong that the club has weathered the Great Depression, World War II and other global conflicts, sweeping societal changes, and the unexpected turns its members' lives often take.

Our club's members have gathered regularly since 1926. Early records reveal that there was some ambivalence regarding the use of the word *modern*. Some members preferred *recent*. From time to time the question still arises: "What is modern literature?" (Additionally, the question "What is literature?" has been raised through the decades, giving members pause and more than once or twice stirring heated exchanges.) An answer shaped by experience seems to be any work of fiction, drama, prose, social commentary, or poetry of enduring quality that has been written within the last five years from the present.

Details of the club's organization were worked out in a constitution adopted in 1931 and revised in 1987, but there seems to be a general consensus not to refer to it unless in dire need. Nevertheless, this club, though its members may joke about haphazardness, delay, or confusion, is, make no mistake about it, thoroughly organized and efficient. Officers and committees are nominated and approved annually. New members are nominated by others, and a closed ballot is held.

The Modern Literature Club, limited to thirty-five active members, meets twice monthly on Tuesday afternoons from September to May, following an academic schedule. Members choose their own books to review, sometimes with anxious trepidation, sometimes with quick and remarkable assuredness. The books are then purchased by the club from its treasury (members pay dues of ten dollars a year), circulated and read, and finally sold at auction in May. Also in May, members receive a copy of the forthcoming year's schedule, detailing titles of books to be reviewed by whom, on what date, and in whose home. Reviewing by any one member is done every other year. If not reviewing, a member is hostessing.

Consistent in the history of the club is a level of review that is both scholarly and lively, but that takes place only after members have enjoyed coffee or tea and accompanying treats, and after the meeting is called to order, minutes read, the treasurer's report heard, and any announcements made. Then the reviewer begins, typically speaking for thirty to forty-five minutes. While it is acceptable to make comments or ask questions during a review, most members wait until the reviewer has concluded and sighed relief, at which time she might hear all manner of comment, a surprising question or two, and perhaps opposing views as a discussion takes form. It is not unusual to hear laughter. Sometimes humorous or anecdotal additions are offered, usually relevant. Word has it that through the years there has been the occasional tiff between members; in most cases these have been quickly resolved.

Along with serious reading, the Modern Literature Club is known for its conviviality. To share the spirit, each spring we have a lovely catered dinner in a member's home for members and their guests. The gathering is made more entertaining by the appearance of someone who is there to do just that—entertain. We've had performers read poetry or prose, deliver an enlightening talk, or stage plays or skits. Often the club has drawn upon local talent, of which there is no shortage, for these memorable evenings. The spring dinners are always gladly anticipated, but the potluck luncheons that grace the beginning and end of the club's year are also attended with congenial delight.

The minutes of the Modern Literature Club are full of stories that illustrate the character of the club members and their loyalty to literature. Attention to one of their determined own was displayed at the very first meeting on February 10, 1926. The women intended to have the literary discussion first and refreshments later. But it was a cold, rainy day, and one of the women arrived wet and shivering. The minutes read, "Refreshments were served first for the comfort of Miss Gray, who walked over a mile in the wind and rain to be with us."

Three years later, the minutes report that the club adopted the outline for literary clubs printed in the May 1929 *Scribners Magazine*. Magazines were exchanged and even reviewed, but not for long. By 1931, the women were back with more solid literary achievements, the serious novel prevailing.

From its beginnings the club has had a strong association with the Fayetteville Public Library, and club business records show that gifts of money were frequently voted. In the early 1940s, when no one was willing to keep the club books at home and be the club librarian, they were allowed to keep the books on a special shelf in the library. In recent years, much thought and discussion has been given to the purchase of memorial books. The tradition of monetary help was revived in 1992 when it was decided the club treasury was "too wealthy," and the majority of the reserves were cheerfully given to a library addition project.

During World War II, economies were suggested. "Mrs. Waterman made a motion that the club in the future *not* serve refreshments. The motion was lost for want of a second." One of the book reviews in 1944 was cancelled, and a female recruiting officer spoke to the group about the Women's Army Corps. Another meeting featured a review of "several experiments in psychology, followed by a test on attitudes toward war." But it was not simply the war and its challenges that diverted the women's attention. At the first club meeting in 1945, three silver baby cups were presented to "club babies."

That the minutes have always been taken seriously is evidenced by occasional comments on their style. In the 1950s it was decided they were too short and lacked the "literary distinction to which the club was accustomed." The minutes lengthened after that until 1992 when the new secretary announced she would not write "reviews of the reviews" and would primarily record the business of the club. It had also been acknowledged that the reading of the "review of the review" took up too much time.

We've tackled questions of gender. Mary Renault's book *The Last of the Wine* inspired a discussion of whether women could write about men and vice versa. In the 1980s a man read about the club in the local paper and applied for membership. The club, feeling only slightly sheepish, turned him down. In 1947 a motion to invite spouses to one meeting a year was turned down. This negative vote was instantly countered by a motion to have an annual dinner for husbands, now the dinner for guests.

The connection between the club and the University of Arkansas has always been strong. Many faculty wives have been members and many members themselves have been connected with the university. The minutes from a guest dinner in February 1960 show that faculty husbands figured prominently in the entertainment: "Mrs. Nichols introduced beatnik poet, Dr. Howard Carter, who read three of his poems accompanied on percussion objects by beatnik musician Dr. Ken Osborne."

Other dinner programs have been more sedate. In 1976 a long-standing member, who was a professor of English and drama, edited and directed the play *The Royal Family* by Kaufman and Ferber. The actors were club members who spent long hours rehearsing and enjoying themselves enormously.

The loyalty factor, both to one another and to the club, has continued to the present day. Despite busy lives and demanding careers, this determination is evident. In 1976 the minutes note that although the hostess had to attend a class at the university law school, the meeting was still held at her home with a friend doing the job of hostess. We are sure the women at that first club meeting would understand and approve.

This club has the perhaps rare distinction of having its records, dating from 1926 to the present, archivally preserved. One can find taped oral histories and a photographic album of portraits of most of the club's members and the minutes of each meeting, beginning with the club's inception, in the Special Collections Division of Mullins Library at the University of Arkansas in Fayetteville. A wealth of club history can be discovered in these careful pages—pages that reflect decades of books and authors reviewed and discussed, business attended to, members mentioned, decisions made—all pointing to the endurance and determination of this group, still so busy and thriving in the hectic 1990s, still composed of members who love the written word and believe in the hope and promise of great literature as well as the fellowship of discourse among friends.

LOL's
DISEASE

Dorothy M. Wilson
Greenwood Village, Colorado

For as long as I remember, I've suffered from a strange disease—one that is universally common, although the World Health Organization hasn't categorized it or given it a name. It is contagious for some people, while in others it lies dormant for years without symptoms. Schools can activate this disease, but because the average classroom teacher is not prepared to handle an epidemic, most schools keep it under control.

I'm not sure when my symptoms—that subtle craving and restlessness—began. I remember a flare-up in junior high that caused me to spend hours in bed, reading all the books I could find.

During adolescence, I controlled the disease with extracurricular activities. The symptoms returned, however, in the last years of college, causing more time in bed and more book reading.

For the next fifteen years I was either in remission or I was too busy working and raising a family to notice any symptoms.

When I returned to graduate school, however, the disease progressed to new heights.

This was a difficult time for my family, and they persuaded me to seek help. My husband suggested a support group. I decided to organize one. I placed an ad in the neighborhood newspaper, on the bulletin board at the supermarket, and at the library. I found many women suffering from the same disease who were also seeking help.

Eight of us began meeting in our homes on the second Tuesday of the month for three hours of group therapy—a group that was to become more important to us than we realized at the time.

That was twenty years ago, and today fifteen of us continue meeting each month, including several original members. A success story? Indeed. We've found a cure for our disease, though we admit we are still dependent on each other for support. We call our affliction LOL's disease, or Love of Learning, and our antidote for it is our Great Books Discussion Group.

We chose the Great Books Reading and Discussion program because it is based on the idea that reading from the great books of our civilization and discussing them with others would help us gain a fuller understanding of the answers in life.

LOL's disease causes a craving for answers, and we were convinced that if we explored the great minds over the centuries, we would find those answers and satisfy our cravings. We found instead that one answer always led to another question and our search would begin again.

We tried to determine why each of us had LOL's disease. Was there a common factor? We found that anyone can be affected at any time—young or old, rich or poor. The average age of our group was forty-five. Over the years, the oldest member was eighty, the youngest thirty. Most of us were college educated, some with graduate degrees. We were all married, or had been. We all had children, and, through the years, grandchildren. Some were working, or had worked, outside the home. Others had not.

We were a diverse group who rarely saw each other between meetings. Our occupations included practicing lawyer, retired teacher, real estate agent, councilwoman, horse trainer. Three were Jewish, two Irish Catholic, one Agnostic, one Christian Scientist, one New Age; others weren't sure. There were more Republicans than Democrats or Independents, but the Democrats were more vocal.

In the beginning we strictly followed the Great Books schedule. Only after many years did we search for new material. We did not use trained leaders, nor did we have coleaders. We took turns leading the discussions. Some of the selections were more difficult than others, but we found we gained from each selection if we patiently plodded our way through. We read the Trilogy on the Nature of Man, "The Search for Meaning," "Becoming Human," and "The Individual and Society." We finished the Modern Adult Series, numbers one through four.

Between questions we drank coffee, talked about our husbands, children, grandchildren, neighborhoods, politics, and religion. Babies were born, marriages ended, illnesses endured, and deaths accepted. Several members moved away and new ones filled their places. At one of our sessions, a member returned from the funeral of her daughter, who had died of lymphoma at age thirty-four. For three hours we cried together.

It was soon after this meeting that we began to suspect there may be a cure for LOL's disease. You see, when one reaches a certain age, after many years of asking questions and trying to find answers, one realizes the truth. Accepting that truth is the cure for LOL's disease. The truth, as the Good Book tells us, can set us free.

What is the truth? The truth is: there are no answers. Or if there are, we mortals are not to know them in this life.

It is also true, however, that a life spent looking for answers with a love of learning is fulfilling. So we will keep our cure to ourselves and continue our group therapy, happily supporting each other in our mutual suffering from LOL's disease.

Our rules for success: We all share a love of learning; we are open to new ideas; we try to be broadminded; we respect others' opinions; we realize that everyone sees the world through her own eyes, and we try to show how we see it or feel it, but we don't try to change others who see it differently; we are not a rigid, formal group; we don't pretend to know it all; we are all different and we like it that way.

BEERS AND DRUM BEATING IN THE KITCHEN

Rodd Zolkos
Chicago, Illinois

When I tell people I belong to a book group, more often than not their response is surprise. Not because I strike them as completely illiterate (I hope), but rather because I'm a man.

Book groups, it seems, are an almost exclusively female undertaking. As a man in a book group, I'm a curiosity. Odd as that seems, I'd have to say my experience bears out the generalization about book groups' membership. My book group-related conversations in the office are typically with women who belong to book groups. After expressing surprise at my participation in a group, they always show keen interest in hearing about my group and what we're reading.

Attempts at similar conversations with my male coworkers don't go very far. The guys I work with don't belong to book groups. They're polite enough to listen, but I'm a journalist by trade—a trained observer—and the heavy glaze that invariably forms over their pupils as I tell them the details of last night's discussion of *Nostromo* clues me in pretty quickly that they're not too interested.

Before this observation skitters too dangerously toward sexism (or is it reverse sexism? My P.C. isn't always what it should be), I've got to note that these same guys are no slouches in the reading department. True, their reading lists always include the daily sports section and *Sports Illustrated* (as do those of many of my women friends), but these guys almost always have a serious book going as well. Fiction, biography, whatever—they're readers. We frequently swap book suggestions or discuss recently read titles. I know these guys could do it.

So why is it when the conversation turns to book group—or in those wilder moments when I actually suggest they attend a session—their attitude isn't one of interest (real or feigned) or even one of confronting an idea once considered and rejected, but instead a sort of patient resignation, an understanding that if they wait long enough the conversation will return to a tongue in which they're conversant? Maybe I should talk about book group louder and more slowly.

Oh, the plight of a man in a book group.

Fortunately, at our monthly meetings I'm not always the only exception to the book group gender rule. At some sessions, if the overall attendance is small and all the current male participants turn out, the group can be evenly split along gender lines. That's three men out of six, and it's rare, but it's an event worth noting, if just to myself, when it occurs.

Other nights, it's just me.

There have been other men in our group during its nearly six-year history, but lack of interest, busy schedules, and personality conflicts have thinned the male ranks. One member even moved to Europe, which was stretching to find a way out if you ask me, though since he moved he has to be commended for participating in some meetings by fax.

Our group has always had a core membership attending nearly every meeting, coupled with less-consistent though equally-enthusiastic-when-present members who can usually be counted on to boost the turnout. While that core shrank for a time (from roughly eight to about three or four), it's since stabilized at a perfectly workable half dozen. With the fringe membership, this can give us a dozen or more at any given meeting. Though some members have drifted away, new blood has joined the group, almost always female.

Not that that's bad. Again, I'll try to steer clear of the rocky shoals of sexism, this time by avoiding the suggestion that there's some sort of intrinsic pleasure in being the lone man in a gathering of well-read women, though I've got no beef.

And I really don't believe our group's female-heavy roster has affected the direction our group has taken with regard to selecting books. While some groups plan their reading a year in advance, ours is done on a meeting-by-meeting basis. The final act of business at our meetings (immediately after the book discussion portion, which can go from forty-five minutes to an hour and a half, and just before the degeneration into free-for-all socializing) is the decision of what to read next and where to discuss it. The book selection is done on a purely consensus basis, an amazing process that usually produces results just as it reaches the point of threatening to meander forever without resolution.

Looking at the titles we've chosen, I can't really say there's a pattern of sexual bias. Authors we've read range from Jane Austen to Ken Kesey, Dashiell Hammett to Virginia Woolf, Toni Morrison to Thomas Mann. We've read Willa Cather and Truman Capote, Flannery O'Connor and William Faulkner, Edith Wharton and Nelson Algren.

We try to be conscious of mixing our mostly classic selections by author's gender, nationality, and time period, but despite our group's female tilt, over our first sixty more or less monthly meetings, we've been top-heavy toward male writers, about two-thirds to one-third.

Nor do I see any inherent bias in the way our group analyzes the books we read. I tend to be one who doesn't believe in such things as "men's books" or "women's books," and likewise don't believe there are likely to be "male" readings versus "female" readings of any particular work. And I think most of the women in our group would agree with me. But darn it, sometimes I feel my views might get a more sympathetic hearing if a few more of the bearded segment of the species were there to back me up.

And, needless to say, that kind of backup would prove invaluable on those occasions when the socializing turns to some member's relationship troubles, and I find myself in the hopeless position of defending my sex in an all-men-are-scum discussion. The best course of action there, experience has shown, is taking the discretion-is-the-better-part-of-valor tack and adjourning to the kitchen to fetch beers.

I guess my final observation on being a man in a book group puts to the lie a little the notion that our group's work is free of any sort of gender bias. It's a little amusement I call the Hemingway-Bellow game after two authors we haven't read in group yet.

The rules are simple. During the book selection portion of the meeting, I suggest a work by Hemingway, then one by Bellow, noting to myself which draws the louder groan. You can't play it too often or you risk getting sullen stares instead of the groans you seek, but from time to time, Hemingway-Bellow can be good book group fun for any man.

I'm not sure how I'd react if I ever did succeed in getting *Henderson the Rain King* chosen as the next month's selection. I guess if nothing else I could be pretty sure of finally attending a book group meeting where men outnumber women. Dramatically. And while I'm sure all my observations would be recognized for their amazing insight, I wonder how long I could continue the dialogue with myself. Of course, if the discussion faltered, there'd always be beers and drum beating in the kitchen.

SO MANY BOOKS, SUCH A LONG TIME: READING TOGETHER FOR EIGHTEEN YEARS

Paula Zurowski, Sarah Booth, Ceinwen Carney,
Roz Hardy, Merry Selk, Karen Davison,
Peggy Aulisio, Susan Powning, Dore Brown,
Judith McKibben, Sheila Levine
Berkeley, California

B erkeley, California, in 1975 was an invigorating place for a woman to be. Nixon had resigned, the pill was available, *Roe v. Wade* had been decided, AIDS was unknown. Women were putting off marriage and children and exploring their identities. Women's groups were rapidly forming—consciousness-raising groups, feminist action groups, radical lesbian groups, women's study groups. Women's issues were in the forefront and classes on women writers and their work were offered everywhere.

The Book Group began as a place for us to explore women's issues through our reading of women's writing. It was a haven where we could explore our feelings and attitudes toward the changing roles of women and men without having to apologize, placate, or yield to a man. The Book Group allowed us to continue to read and analyze books even though our college classes were over. We would choose our own reading list, structure the discussion topics, and focus the reading to please ourselves. We were leaderless, but not without leadership, and

we found that making group decisions was difficult but rewarding. We've learned much along the way—about ourselves, about group dynamics, about making, breaking, and
changing rules, about tolerance for others' views.

By far the greatest challenge we faced in the early years was
selecting and integrating new members. We all had friends
who liked to read; the question was, did they have what it took
to be in the group? We asked for serious commitment: read
every book (cover to cover) and come to every meeting (and
those were the days of weekly meetings). This strict requirement wasn't always easy to enforce.

> One former member repeatedly flaunted our read-or-stay-
> home rule. As a founding member who believed that this
> rule was critical to the group's integrity, I was increasingly
> exasperated each time she announced that she didn't have
> time to read but came because she loved the meetings. I felt
> she had reached the height of audacity when, while hosting
> her own book, she admitted that she hadn't read the book
> before nominating it and had since only managed to get
> through fifty pages, so *we'd* have to tell *her* what it was
> about. As I rushed out of the room to hyperventilate, the
> rest of the group rose to the occasion and eloquently
> cleared up her confusion about The Rule. —*PZ*

Other confrontations sparked by "The Rule" left more
painful memories. In the end, members who could not keep up
with our rigorous reading schedule quit the group. Those who
remained formed a solid core of dedicated readers.

Today there are eleven of us—four from the founding year,
six from the next ten years, and one seven-year fledgling.
There have been many changes since our beginning, but one
constant—we still insist that members finish the book. The
type of in-depth discussion we aim for isn't possible without a
thorough reading of the book, and it's annoying to have to
explain the plot to delinquent readers.

As we've become busier over the years, we've relaxed our
reading schedule. We now meet every other week. We've also

become more flexible, and "commitment" has taken on a different meaning. We no longer look askance at members who miss meetings or take leaves of absence; we just try to stay in touch and hope they'll return soon. When the group began, most members were in their twenties, single, childless, and living in apartments decorated with beanbag chairs. Now most of us are in our forties, married, parents of young children, and homeowners. Although in most ways we are very similar— white, college-educated, middle-class, working women—we feel our differences.

> Not being a mother, not owning a home, I'm very aware of how our lives have changed. Sometimes I feel that everyone has moved forward but me, but that's when I'm measuring on a limited, traditional scale that doesn't have much to do with how I've chosen to live my life. Of the eleven members, only four of us don't have kids, and I sometimes grow tired of the talk about schools and day care. But I enjoy the kids themselves, who always strike me as remarkably cute, smart, and much bigger than the last time I saw them. It's just a little odd to look around and find that my cohorts marched off without me while I was at my dance class.
>
> —KD

Still the warmth, security, and pride of the group have created compelling bonds. We've become fixtures in each others' lives. When we jointly attend parties, dinners, weddings, and relatives' funerals, strangers come up to us and say, "Oh, you're one of the *book group* members." It's a good feeling.

Nominating a Book Is a Serious Business

As our lives have changed, not surprisingly, our book choices have followed suit. In what seems a flash of years, we've gone from *Looking for Mr. Goodbar* to *The Silent Passage: Menopause*, from the young adults in *Goodbye, Columbus* to the middle-aged children of *Patrimony*, struggling with how to say good-bye to our failing parents. We used to relish long Victorian novels, but the demands of children, careers, and, well, life have made shorter books increasingly appealing.

Although one of our members who is interested in classical literature led us from *The Iliad* through the Greek tragedies and up to the New Testament, for the most part we're readers of nineteenth- and twentieth-century literature. A recent (and idiosyncratic) poll of our favorite books demonstrates how eclectic our reading has been. Our top choices were: Calvino's *If on a Winter's Night a Traveler*, Chase's *During the Reign of the Queen of Persia*, Durrell's *The Alexandria Quartet*, Hulme's *The Bone People*, Kundera's *The Unbearable Lightness of Being*, Levi's *Survival in Auschwitz*, Tolstoy's *Anna Karenina*, and Wolfe's *The Bonfire of the Vanities*.

Our method of choosing a book list has stayed much the same over the years. About every six months, we devote an evening to nominating, voting on, and scheduling our upcoming reading. Each member nominates two books she has read, presenting a short description of plot and an explanation of the potential value of reading and discussing the book (threats, begging, and tears are allowed). Although we may nominate a book in hardcover, we wait to discuss it until it appears in paperback.

Originally we considered the entire list of proposed books and voted, by secret ballot, for our top choices (usually half the list). But often at least one member would have both books rejected, which meant she had to facilitate another member's nomination. (Imagine suggesting *A Mother and Two Daughters* and having to present *Moby-Dick* instead.) Now we listen to all the nominations and then choose one book from each person, still using a written ballot. Dates of the meetings are then set up and houses assigned. To some, nominating a book is a serious business.

Once you nominate a book, it's yours forever. If it's well received, you want full credit, forever. If it's a flop, it's a permanent source of embarrassment. I nominated *Death*

Kit by Susan Sontag and only two people could bring themselves to finish it, and one of them said it gave her a headache. As the three of us sat down to discuss the book, I wished I'd never pulled it off the shelf. —*PZ*

I've finally learned not to nominate a book with great personal meaning, because I can't stand it when people end up hating it. Almost invariably those special books resonate for me in some way that's not transferable. —*KD*

Our first book was *The Little Disturbances of Man* by Grace Paley. We began 1993 with *Backlash* by Susan Faludi. Perhaps we'll discover how far we've come in these eighteen years.

Better Understanding the Work and Ourselves

To us, a good book discussion is one that strikes a balance between examining a book as a piece of writing (its structure, place in literary tradition, style, etc.) and relating it to our lives. At the beginning of each meeting we schmooze for about twenty minutes, and then the facilitator gives a brief biography of the author. We like idiosyncratic details about authors and try to find (or invent) similarities between their lives and their books. Most biographical information is from *Contemporary Authors* and *Contemporary Literary Criticism*, although one of us once found a brief article on Nadine Gordimer in *People* magazine after she won the Nobel—it made her sound and look like a pop star.

After the bio, the facilitator chooses among various topics concerning the book to encourage the best possible discussion. Some facilitators reel off a list of topics at the outset (which results in other members looking cross-eyed). Some anxious facilitators begin by asking, "So, did you like it?" Usually a slight prod in any direction is enough to evoke discussion. The facilitator is also supposed to keep the discussion on track and to steer members gently away from lengthy digressions, a common occurrence given that we are women of strong opinions.

We save professional reviews for last, and researching and reading reviews is, again, the facilitator's job. The goal of presenting reviews is to further discussion or to illuminate our understanding of the book (or to obfuscate, e.g., "these characters . . . were thwarted in their violent passions and had their momentary epiphanies of glory in precisely this manner and no other." Say what?). We look for stimulating critique, not plot summaries. For established authors, critical commentary might replace reviews.

Over the years, we have egotistically, yet truthfully, found that we are as profound as most reviewers. Actually, reviews are often the cause of much hilarity. When a reviewer is particularly hard on a book without just cause, we snidely wonder if maybe he or she had a manuscript rejected by the book's publisher. Reviews from popular magazines like *Newsweek* tend to use a fill-in-the-blank format and always comment on how the author seems to be "chasing personal demons." It's a real clue to a book's (non)success, or to a facilitator's lack of research, when we are reduced to hearing brief reviews from *Publishers Weekly* and *Library Journal*.

Lest the facilitator's job sound too onerous, only about an hour of preparation time is required (sometimes that hour is spent trying to find a parking place near the library). In turn, the group members, out of courtesy to the facilitator, are supposed to be prepared to discuss the book, whether by reading it close enough to the day of the discussion to remember it fully, or by finishing it far enough in advance to think about it before the group meets. Although we have tried to move away from the idea that a book "belongs" to the facilitator, it's a burden we've all felt when our book has been disliked.

> I presented a book that some members hated intensely and attacked ferociously—*A Stricken Field* by Martha Gellhorn. During the discussion, the group got into some pretty serious verbal blows. One person who hated it was relentlessly critical, while someone else said she thought it was a

work of genius. That was the most uncomfortable discussion I remember, and I felt my integrity as a presenter attacked. A few calls were made afterward with apologies.

—*PA*

In contrast, although it's emotionally gratifying to have a book that everyone *adores*, the discussion can be pretty shallow—sometimes an extended if enthusiastic repetition of "I loved the part when . . ."

The best discussions are lively and fluid—differences of opinion and interpretation are energetically debated, and everyone has something to say. With the firm guidance of the facilitator, we can be led to examine a book's literary qualities, particularly if there is some innovation or complexity in the plot, structure, voice, writing style, or other element. Our different readings of the symbolism in *Paris Trout*, for example, generated a surprisingly spirited debate. With other books, especially nonfiction, the subject matter provides the biggest conversational boost. Nearly every discussion is grounded in the personal—in our own experiences and points of view. If we have been successful in probing the book's various dimensions, if we have listened to the book and to each other, we come away with a better understanding of both the work and ourselves.

I have occasionally arrived at the meeting ready to pounce on the book, and I do. I hated Toni Morrison's *Beloved* and wouldn't have stuck with it if I hadn't been reading it for group. But I left with a far greater appreciation of the work after listening to everyone else's comments and watching a videotaped interview with Morrison. —*SL*

The Teas We Drink

For years each member acted as facilitator, host, and dessert chef for her own book. But as the tasks of searching out reviews and author bios, cleaning the house, making or shopping for dessert, quieting the children, shooing the cats, and leading the discussion became a bit overwhelming, we've taken to facilitating our own book at another's house, with a third person providing dessert.

The dessert tray usually features a sweet treat—cake, pie, cookies, chocolate—although some diet-conscious members have lobbied for healthier fare. We accompany the food with decaffeinated tea, an occasional bottle of wine, and a rare cup of coffee. Changes in the times have been reflected in the teas we drink—Female Toner, PMS Tea, Throat Coat (but, alas, nothing to allay the misery of those allergic to cats).

Offering dessert is an extension of hospitality, symbolic of our connection as a social as well as intellectual community. For some it provides an opportunity to be creative. And on occasion it is part of the incentive to come to group.

Off-Nights

Within the first year, we realized that gathering weekly for a book discussion was too ambitious. We wanted the contact with each other, but the strict reading schedule was turning the group into drudgery for some. Membership turnover was greatest in those early years. Our solution was to convert one of our monthly book nights into an "off-night," a meeting night without a specific book scheduled.

In the past eighteen years we have held five hundred book discussion meetings and more than 130 off-nights. For close to half these off-nights, we discussed a variety of topics such as rape, aging, money, food. Each evening's facilitator took responsibility for distributing pertinent articles and discussion ideas in advance and then leading the meeting. We shared our attitudes and feelings and got to know each other in a way we couldn't at book meetings.

We spent another forty off-nights on the town, usually in Berkeley, attending plays, movies, and a few lectures. We also engaged in writing projects, read plays aloud, and held social events, including seders and bridal showers. As new members came into the group, we devoted evenings to exchanging our autobiographies. And some of our most interesting off-nights were those attended by authors—Elizabeth Fischel, Sheila Ballantyne, Arlene Blum, Lauren Elder, Susan Dunlap, and Ernest Callenbach, the only male ever invited to the group.

Off-nights are not currently scheduled, but the concept is so ingrained that we are able to get into the mood at a moment's notice. Our most recent off-night was to discuss how to organize this essay.

Tenth Anniversary, One Year Later

To celebrate the group's tenth anniversary, we went away for a weekend together. However, because it took a year to plan the event, finding a date that worked for all of us, and designing and printing group sweatshirts, we held our first group retreat for our *eleventh* anniversary.

We have managed to get away three times since then. We always choose a spot along the California coast, where there is plenty of opportunity for hiking and hot-tubbing, and sometimes swimming and tennis. An extravagant Saturday night dinner is the highlight. The necessary afterlude is a fiercely battled round or two of charades.

On our first weekend we wrote a novella (starring Reita Booker). Saturday morning each of us received a chapter number, opening sentence, cast of characters, and deadline. We ended the weekend on a light note as we read our chapters aloud over Sunday brunch, laughing at Reita's adventures and personality changes.

Our retreats are always relaxing and fun, though there is never enough time to do all that we'd like to. Nor is there ever enough time for a real book discussion amidst all the competing items on the agenda—like sitting in the hot tub.

A Reading Family

What makes a voluntary group thrive for almost eighteen years? Certainly what binds us is our love of reading and the unusual thrill of knowing it's not a solitary pursuit—that there are ten others reading the same book at the same time who can't wait to talk to each other about it. For some of us, the group also represents a legitimate evening away from the family. For others, it's a way to keep an intellectual, literary life going amidst the duties of writing company reports, running a business, or grading school papers. For some, meeting every other week is an easy way to check in with friends whose life paths have diverged from ours.

Each individual's commitment to the group is what makes it cohere and continue to exist. And it's about that commitment and what it means that we've had raging arguments in the past: rules made and broken about how often you had to be at meetings, how thorough your preparation as a facilitator had to be, whether you had to finish the book to attend. We haven't had one of those discussions for a while, perhaps because we now trust each others' engagement with the group. The group has a life of its own, an energy that's the product of each of our commitments— it's eerie.

Commitment seems to me to be more of an approach to taking the books seriously and thinking about stories and ideas before the meeting. My other sense of commitment is trusting other members' obvious regard for a book. Even if I don't like the book, I feel a commitment to read it and think about it because someone else has cared about it.

—JM

Reading is a passion; I need the connection to the group to keep my intellectual life going. *—RH*

The Book Group is my reading family. Like any family we have our traditions and rituals and a few skeletons in the closet. We have our share of tiffs, hurt feelings, and personality clashes. We tolerate quirks, know weaknesses, tease each other, and can anticipate reactions—to books or ideas. We laugh a lot, challenge one another, and listen to each other. We take each other seriously. After eighteen years, my commitment to the group is a given because the experience is so intellectually and personally rewarding. It's wonderful to have a place to go where I can begin a story with "Remember when . . ." and laugh all over again. —*PZ*

During the past ten years, a group fantasy with many variations has taken form at our gatherings. It goes something like this. All eleven of us co-own and live in a Victorian house somewhere close to or in Berkeley. Now in our seventies and eighties, we spend our leisure hours either reading for the next group, which once again meets weekly, or reminiscing about our colorful past, which includes our twenty-fifth anniversary trip to Italy at the turn of the century. We now have the time to hit the streets for all those causes that attracted us in our youth. And, at last, we each write our novel, and one by one, when published, we lay ourselves open to the scrutiny of the most discerning group of women readers this side of Strawberry Creek—yes, the Book Group, established 1975.

THE POETS ARE COMING

Peggy Heinrich
Westport, Connecticut

We are a group of poetry lovers who live in Connecticut's Fairfield County. Most of us are from Westport, a town fifty miles north of New York City. Many of us write poetry, some are English teachers, and some have been editors for local newspapers and small press magazines. Many of the founding members originally met in a poetry writing workshop. About a quarter of our group members are men.

Our goal in forming the group was to increase our appreciation and understanding of poetry—those too-often enigmatic stacks of lines on a page—and to become more familiar with the work of contemporary as well as classic poets.

Every other Monday from 3:30 to 6:00, we assemble in a member's living room to read and discuss the work of a single poet. Whether as few as three attend or as many as ten, each meeting is rewarding, enough to have kept us going uninterrupted for fifteen years. We have no officers and no official name. We commonly refer to ourselves as "The Poetry Group."

We try to limit our socializing to half an hour, but it's difficult. As we sip our coffee or herbal tea, nibble cheese and crackers or an apple, we share our thoughts about a recent poetry reading or art show, about a book read or film seen. We chat about the latest events—the election, a vacation, a new job, a wedding, a divorce. Sitting in a circle, we move on to news of the poetry world: Mary Oliver won the National Book Award, Galway Kinnell's giving a reading at Fairfield University, Mona Van Duyn's our new Poet Laureate. On a more personal level, we trade news of a poem published or a grant won by a member of the group.

At last we settle down and pass around copies of the featured work. Today it's Irish poet Eavan Boland. Janet, who suggested Boland, fills us in on her background and reads the first poem, "Object Lessons," aloud. As she finishes, someone emits a hum of approval, someone else a groan of bewilderment. We resist making specific comments until we've had a chance to reread the poem to ourselves. Finally someone breaks the silence with an opinion about the poem's metaphor ("the broken coffee mug represents the couple's breakup"). Another member calls attention to the sounds ("note all the words with hard 'k' sounds: black, silk, hawk, kiss, cake"). A phrase is cited for its fresh, vivid language ("the way land looks before disaster," "a kitchen full of chaos"). Comments are casual and often lead to laughter. Or they turn serious when a member's personal problem surfaces, called to mind by the poem's message. After reading several more poems, we're in agreement in our admiration for and enjoyment of Boland's work and rate her among the better poets we've studied.

We don't always agree. Opinions may vary about a poet's talent and skill or about a poem's meaning. Whether a poem ended on a hopeful note or one of despair is a question that often divides us. One person may rate a poet the best since Wallace Stevens, while another may question why his or her work was ever published. Someone may point out sexual symbols ("the whole poem is a metaphor for a phallus"), or religious imagery ("the figure on the wheel is Christ-like"). We consider each interpretation, accepting or rejecting it according to our backgrounds and biases.

At the end of each meeting, we choose the poet for the upcoming session, someone volunteers his or her home, someone offers to make selections and copies. This last is usually Janet, one of our original members. Janet, an English professor and poet, is well versed in the field of poetry, often discovers new poets for us, excels at spotting mythological references, and has access to a copying machine.

Cynthia, who founded the group, is our New Testament expert, shedding light on poems dealing with the annunciation or the stations of the cross. She introduced us to David Whyte, a British poet with a spiritual bent, whom she encountered when she joined one of his poetry/walking tours in England.

Barrett, who recently spent two weeks at a Dublin poetry workshop, brought back books by several exceptional Irish poets unknown to us, including Paula Meehan and Derek Mahon.

Artists Ann and Barbara G. are particularly sensitive to a poem's visual imagery, as is photographer Barbara L. They add another dimension to our insights by reminding us of the ways certain aspects of a poem compare with those in the visual arts.

Lou, who teaches a course in Myth and Bible at the local high school, enlightens us on mythological or biblical references, pointing out lines that allude to Moses' stutter, the fate of Narcissus, or the geography of Dante's underworld.

A physicist and businessman, as well as an avid reader and writer of poetry, Peter offers analytical and intuitive insights along with a knowledge of German, which has been helpful when we've read such poets as Rilke, Goethe, and Schiller.

Ginny brings in copies of poems from *The New Yorker*. She's introduced us to work by Dave Smith, Dana Gioia, Emily Grosholz, and others.

Freya, a children's book author who died this year, is missed for many reasons, including her enthusiasm for a startling image, a fresh metaphor, a meaningful message.

If several poets are suggested for the next session, we line them up in advance, assigning responsibility for each to various group members. The *New York Times Book Review*, the *New York Review of Books*, and magazines like the *American Poetry Review* alert us to possible subjects. Members who buy poetry books or borrow them from the library make copies of selected poems for future sessions.

The member responsible for a particular poet selects six to ten poems, makes sufficient copies, and is prepared with brief biographical material. One advantage of a poetry group over a book group is that there's no need for members to read the work in advance since poems are usually short enough to deal with on the spot. If we run out of time to cover all the selections or if enthusiasm merits, we often continue a poet's work at our next meeting.

Getting started can be a problem. It requires shifting from a social mood to a more contemplative one. But that's when our group is at its brightest and what we assemble for—that rare out-of-one's-self state attainable when we're struggling to understand on an intuitive level as well as a rational, intellectual one—when we're in touch with words and thoughts born in another's imagination.

To start, one member reads a poem aloud, the group discusses it, then another member reads the second poem, and so on. We simply move around our circle taking turns as readers. During the discussions, we focus on the following questions: What is the poem saying? What are its outstanding lines or phrases? After we've read several poems, we consider the poet's attitude (pessimistic, optimistic?), style (surreal, lyrical, narrative?), and obsessions (nature, childhood?). Does the poet call to mind other poets, writers, artists? If it deserves consideration, we comment on the poem's form, rhyming pattern, line breaks, language, and so on.

We do have a few flexible rules that we've found useful. We speak from a personal point of view, as blanket statements about a poem's meaning or value tend to intimidate shier members, and, as with anything else, no one is privy to the truth of a poem. A variety of opinions can be valid.

We try to avoid digression. A poem can trigger a childhood memory, a film or book that someone has read, an association with a person or event. This is fine, as long as the commentary doesn't ramble far afield.

We always have a dictionary handy. Poets excel in accurate word selection, and their choices are often challenging. A dictionary will shed light on obscure usage.

One reason our group has survived so long is the compatibility of its members. No one resorts to bullying or seeks to dominate. We consider each others' opinions with an open mind, express our thoughts from a personal point of view, and resist making strong statements that imply knowledge of absolute truth.

Occasionally a new person has joined who monopolizes discussion, talks about him- or herself, or makes irrelevant comments. Strangely, such people vanish after a meeting or two. I'm not sure about the dynamics that cause this—we're never rude or nasty. Perhaps it is our unresponsiveness to their input that discourages any interest they may have in us. On the other hand, more recent members like Barrett, Lou, and Virginia have blended in without causing a ripple of dissension.

The group process enriches our understanding of each poet's work. Together we give a poem the time and concentration it requires. Too frequently, when we read a poem on our own, we misjudge it, perhaps because we fail to crack the code and grasp its message or because we under- or overrate its skill.

When I began with the group fifteen years ago, I found poetry baffling. I was used to the more logical, realistic writing of journalism and fiction that imparts information or narrates a story. I was unprepared for a poem's open spaces, its highly compressed message that omits as much as it offers. Thanks to The Poetry Group, I now approach a poem more confidently, better equipped to enter its landscape of the spirit and emotions.

I generally leave each meeting expanded by the results of our effort, enriched by the poet's language and my glimpse of the way his or her mind works. As I head home, powerful lines and images continue to resonate along nerve endings, or wherever it is that seeds of art take root, and I'm grateful to these writers who have generously shared their thoughts, memories, and dreams.

It was Ginny who informed us, during a session at her house, that earlier that day, when she had rushed into the local cheese shop to purchase snacks for our meeting, she had announced to the owner with great excitement, "The poets are coming! The poets are coming!"

"Not all of us are poets," one of our more literal members reminded her.

Ginny hesitated a moment, then said, "You might as well be. And what about that?" She pointed to the pile of poems waiting to be distributed. "The poets have arrived!"

It's true. The poets have been coming to our homes for years, and, it is hoped, will continue to be our guests for a long, long time.

THE
SISTERHOOD

Mary E. Toole
Chicago, Illinois

In October 1982, forty African-American women united in the spirit of friendship and fellowship to form the Sisterhood, a book discussion group. Books written or edited by African-American women, with few exceptions, are read monthly. Sunday meetings are held on a rotating basis in the homes of group members. Each member is asked to bring a dish or beverage to serve four. The exception is our annual champagne-catered celebration of the Sisterhood. At this time we reflect and affirm with our own words. The poem "Sistahs" represents my recollection and affirmation of the Sisterhood. Within the poem, twenty-one book titles are remembered—recalled—recollected in the spirit shared by my Sistahs.

SISTAHS

We are—
Sunday Ladies
Four hour Mamas
of "Lit."

From Breaking Bread to
Gourmet Salads of
J. California Cooper
We know *Family* and
Struggle with—

The Matter is Life

Embracing our wounds from
Middle Passage
Faith and the Good Thing
We Invented Lives—
Wept in our Brass Beds
Mad at Miles.

We couldn't
"Wait to Exhale"
Hearts pounded
Pressures soared
With Memories of Kin . . .

Disappearing Acts
Sometimes Passing or
Jumping in Quicksand
Yelling, "Sistah"

Sistah, Sistah
Who knows—
Every Goodbye Ain't Gone.
That, There is Confusion.
Breaking Ice,
Imploring Balm in Gilead,
Reading Lemon Swamp and
Other Places.

Sundays cry out from
The Temple of My Familiar,
Sistah!
And, I shall not be moved.

Daughters of the Dust
Sistahs
Sunday Ladies—
Four hour Mamas
Possessing the Secret of Joy

Sistahs—
Kindred Spirits
Nurturing our
Insides from the inside
Our souls to keep

Sistahs!

CLAREMONT PARK BOOK CLUB

JoEllen Brean
Berkeley, California

Could the Claremont Park Book Club survive its seventy-fourth year—a year of devastation and terror for seventeen of its members? Could a long-established women's group use the strength of its history and the intent of its founding members to recover from the fire storm of October 20, 1991?

Those are questions the original members probably couldn't even imagine when the club was first organized in 1917. Its twenty-three members were chosen from the area east of Claremont Avenue in Berkeley, south of Fish Ranch Road, and north of the Oakland city line, an area that includes what is known as the "Hiller Property." When that area was annexed by Oakland, it remained part of our district. The area from which members are drawn was kept small to facilitate the distribution of books among members. This is the area hit by the fire storm.

Originally, the club had two purposes: to keep abreast of current literature: and to aid the war effort by knitting for the Red Cross. To fulfill the first purpose, the club purchased enough books to circulate two books twice a month to each member. At the end of the year, two weeks were reserved to gather the books that had been read and to distribute new ones to the members. When someone resigned, a new member was invited by the membership committee. Two current members had to endorse any prospective member. A reading from or review of a book was given at each meeting. To fulfill the second purpose, the club members gathered their needles and yarn and began to knit.

The club met on the second and fourth Monday of each month from October through May, with single meetings in September, November, December, and January. In the early 1920s, the members decided to double their ranks. The membership chairman called on the ladies invited to join. She left her calling card and wore white kid gloves.

In the early years, each member brought her own lunch, while the hostess provided tea and coffee, nuts, olives, and other relishes. Gradually the hostess began providing cookies, then salad, then sandwiches, and step by step, lunch, prepared by the hostess, two cohostesses, and a paid helper, became part of the meeting.

In those early years, club members were also given two books by lot at the end of the year. Book prices having risen dramatically, an annual book auction was introduced and is now used as a means of meeting expenses. The auction has proven profitable and entertaining.

The meetings were held then, as they are today, in the homes of members, and guests are invited only to the December meeting and the last meeting in May. The meetings with guests take place at one of the larger homes or at a private club. Originally there was an occasional meeting to which husbands were invited.

In the 1920s and 1930s, some of the members' large homes were demolished and the land they stood on divided into lots where many homes have since been built. Club members had loved going to these spacious homes for the annual meetings and still remember with enthusiasm the forty-six-room Taylor mansion and the equally spacious Hines home. Although many large houses have disappeared, we are still fortunate to have most of our meetings in members' homes.

Through the years, the membership has included musicians, dramatists, artists, physicians, authors, lecturers, garden enthusiasts, librarians, business experts, teachers, and environmental activists. The membership has increased by the addition of associate members, women who have moved out of the book distribution area. The number of associates is limited to twelve.

The changes that have occurred through the years have not altered the main purpose set by our founding members seventy-four years ago. The mechanics of book distribution, meetings, and adding new members still work well.

And it was those mechanics that served us in October 1991 when a fire in the Berkeley-Oakland hills destroyed the homes and belongings of hundreds of people, including seventeen members of the Claremont Park Book Club. The Book Club membership is made up of forty-six women who live within the area that the fire storm hit and twelve women who formerly lived in that area. The police ordered all residents of the area to be evacuated. We left not knowing when or even if we would be allowed to return to our homes. When we did return, we saw mile after mile of blackened emptiness.

None of our members was among the twenty-two people killed by the fire, but all had friends among those twenty-two. The stories we shared were horrifying. One member jumped from a deck and ran down the street in bare feet with her hair on fire. Most of the seventeen lost everything.

The Book Club seemed unimportant compared to helping the victims of the fire. And yet we decided to try to keep some semblance of continuity. The house where we were scheduled to meet had been destroyed. A substitute was offered. We met, as scheduled, thirteen days after the fire.

Typically, thirty or so members attend meetings. We expected less than that at this meeting. We had forty-six attendees. Almost all of the fire victims came—some in borrowed clothes, others in clothes they had just bought. They came with faces strained with shock. They came to be with their friends and neighbors, to be comforted and to give reassurance to those whose lives were intact. Somehow, those of us who had not been burned out needed to be comforted by those who had.

Varying degrees of friendship exist among our members. But on that day we were all close, greeting each other with subdued voices, strengthened with joy and relief. Many hugged silently.

The Claremont Park Book Club still meets ten times a year, from September through May. We have lunch at noon, and at one o'clock a member presents a book review. At two o'clock we say good-bye. But now we know there is a need, a reason for the club to meet. Not, as originally intended seventy-four years ago, to keep abreast of current literature and to knit for the Red Cross, but to affirm our concern, affection, and support for each other.

The ties that bind us are an interest in books and friendship. The second Monday after the October fire storm, that second tie became paramount. The club survived its seventy-fourth year, became stronger because of its members' ordeals, and celebrated its seventy-fifth anniversary with thanks and great hope for the future.

IF I READ ENOUGH BOOKS, WILL I SOMEDAY HAVE BEEN EVERYWHERE?

Cindra Halm
Minneapolis, Minnesota

We are six women battling winter in Minnesota with books. Knee-deep snow, subzero temperatures, icy roads and sidewalks, and wind chills can make one feel isolated even in a cultural mecca like the Twin Cities. For some of us northern folk, winter sports means lifting a book from shelf to lap and turning pages slowly, deliberately. Some people take cross-country ski treks and annual outings to the Ice Palace in St. Paul. I have my books—and my book club.

Picture this: a turquoise-colored Deco couch, a woolen afghan, a cup of chamomile tea, a book. And these: a fireplace, children in bed, hot chocolate, a book. Or this: a wall full of plants, a fluffy grey cat, a book. The same book in at least half a dozen homes, and who knows how many more? Dotted throughout the city, we live in our own lighted rooms, connected like stars in a constellation by a common set of words. Later, when we gather in one of those rooms to discuss the story, and our stories, words are what motivate us, join us, keep us warm.

Of course, winter ends eventually, even in Minnesota, and we continue to read. One of my brightest memories of book club is a summer one—picnicking on the banks of the Mississippi River, discussing *The Adventures of Huckleberry Finn*, spitting watermelon seeds at the water. Basking in Huck's abandon, we could almost believe that we, too, floated on a raft, moving with the current of conversation and the curve of the setting sun. No matter that we were northerners, sitting at the top of the river, and that Huck and Jim were southerners moving farther south. The river, same to us in some knowledge and experience, made us kin.

If only we could move every book into our blood that way—sipping wine in a French village while discussing *Madame Bovary*, or hiking in Virginia's Blue Ridge Mountains to talk about *Pilgrim at Tinker Creek*. As it is, I read books to trade places, or to become more deeply rooted in some same place, whether that place is geographical, emotional, spiritual, or tonal. If I read enough books, will I someday have been everywhere?

We six have been avid readers since childhood. Some would find our demographic profile bland, for in many ways our similarities to one another are great. We are each white, thirty to forty years old, heterosexual, college educated, middle class. Two are mothers. Four are married. The group originated in 1985 out of Odegard Books of Minneapolis, an independent bookstore in which most of the members worked. People have come and gone. Friends of members are, from time to time, recruited or admitted, with six being the maximum and ideal enrollment for ease of scheduling.

The current incarnation first converged in 1989. I was at that time one of the newest members, having recently moved back to Minneapolis. Within this homogeneous group, our occupations and interests vary—law student, freelance writer, quilter, regional sales manager, art conservator, graphic designer, waitress, marathon runner, child care provider, sculptor, saxophone player, antiques collector, swimmer, poet, traveler, reader, reader, reader, reader, reader, reader.

Here's how our group works. We convene once a month. The person who has selected that month's title hosts the meeting in her home. In our club, providing a delicious treat is almost as important as choosing a challenging text. The host is also responsible for providing background information about the author and the chosen book. Usually the books are fiction, though a few have been essays (*The Solace of Open Spaces* by Gretel Erlich) or biography (*The Woman Warrior* by Maxine Hong Kingston). We are interested in reading literary works, whether classic or contemporary, books that engage the mind and the heart, stories that encompass history and timelessness, place and placement.

The meetings are casual and conversational. We talk first about ourselves and our lives during the previous month. There's a lot of catching up to do. We eat and drink. Usually, the host, or some pertinent comment, will guide the discussion toward the book. At times the talk is argumentative, even heated. At times there is a unanimous reverence for the skill of the author or the direction of a character. There is never a lack of words about the words that brought us together.

Toward the end of the meeting, about four hours later, we consult our calendars for the next available Sunday night. Often scheduling is difficult. Sometimes one or another hasn't had time to read the book. Even so, our book club is like a clock ticking around the obstacles and necessary functions of daily life. It has survived, with flexibility and humor, for seven years. There is no end in sight.

For me, the book club has a grounding influence. Sharing conversation about books and about myself on a regular basis with wonderful women is inspiring and comforting. The group has become a priority and a sanctuary. It has carved its own monthly orbit, like the moon or menstruation. Reading can be a solitary experience, but having a group makes it a communal one. I'm doing something positive for myself by being involved. Part social hour, literary guild, gossip fence, and philosophical roundtable, the club travels from month to month, from home to home, gathering momentum and history. And because I belong to it, I can go anywhere and still be home.

WRITERS ON READING, SARATOGA STYLE

F. R. Lewis
Albany, New York

Once we've settled on *Song of Solomon*—available in paper, a must—I begin, as is my habit, to research beyond the rational, photocopying on poster-sized sheets summarized reviews from *American Authors, Black American Authors, Current Biography*, and *Book Review* something or other, as well as several volumes of literary scholarship on Toni Morrison. I even find a few of her own well-chosen words, a few good quotes, I think, words to stimulate or close off discussion. I secure interesting-sounding titles from bibliographic listings through interlibrary loan. And, oh yes, I read the book again. Twice. The month is August. On September 25, I will not go unfortified to the Saratoga Springs Public Library to be reading group leader.

Meeting monthly in the library's community room—in a community of just over 20,000—the reading group is in its sixth season. Many of the original participants continue to attend more or less regularly, a corps of twelve, drawn not only by their love of reading or, especially in the case of thirtysomethings with young children, a need for an intellectual night out, but also by the format that has evolved.

In the beginning, thinking that a reading group with somebody knowledgeable to lead it was something her library should have, Linda Bullard, who coordinates adult programs, "hired" poet, prose writer, and teacher William "Kit" Hathaway. He led the fledgling group through a topical series, "Wealth and Poverty in the American Novel."

The first year, as in every year since, reading group selections included the classic and the modern, the well known if previously unread, the unknown, and the "I never would read this otherwise" both known and unknown. Only the idea of a unifying topic was dropped, neither of the next two year-long leaders—short story writer Beth Weatherby and Jennifer Armstrong, a writer of novels and stories for children and young adults—being interested in continuing the practice.

The library provided a small honorarium—fifty dollars per session, rising to sixty-five during Armstrong's tenure. Hathaway had come to the library seeking work. The other year-long occupants had in turn attended a session conducted by her predecessor. Armstrong, for example, was captivated by Marilynne Robinson's *Housekeeping* and was inspired to arrange discussions of some of her favorite books. For each, however, running the reading group sessions proved too much work for too little money.

Wanting to keep the group running as a part of her library's menu of programs for adults, Bullard revamped her series and looked for money outside the library budget. For three years, the library has received grant money from the New York State Council on the Arts to run the reading series year-round. Each session is conducted by a local writer—that is, a writer from within a fifty-mile radius.

Bullard describes her method for selecting writers for her reading group as "kind of sneaky." For another of her public programs, "Writer's Night," a monthly event featuring local authors reading from new work, she periodically sends out a call for resumes and writing samples.

"From that group I look for people who have been published, although that's preferred rather than necessary. Teaching experience is a plus," Bullard says.

Last February, writers on Bullard's "A" list received a letter on library letterhead stating, "Enclosed is a description of the reading group at the Saratoga Springs Public Library. Thanks to the New York State Council on the Arts, the library is able to offer $125 for leadership for one evening. I have openings in May. Please contact me if you are . . . interested."

I was interested.

According to the grant proposal, the guest writer begins the reading group session with a brief talk on or reading from his or her work. Then, after explaining the reason she or he chose the book to be discussed, writer and readers discuss that book.

In addition to being an admirer of Toni Morrison's writing since I discovered her on the pages of *Redbook* magazine, I had studied with her during her tenure at State University at Albany. I thought *Song of Solomon* displayed the broad range of her creative and intellectual gifts, her emotional energy. And not only would the group hear my voice reading my story, but I could play for them, on audiotape, Morrison reading the first chapter of her book.

"No format of this kind can be rigid," the grant proposal says. "Presumably, analysis of the book selected and the guest writer's feeling about writing become evident and reflect upon his or her writing . . . to the benefit of the group. . . . The presence of guest writers . . . invigorates and stimulates the group, draws more people and provides a means for the library to support local writers."

The library continues to cover the costs of news releases, publishing and mailing fliers, and buying eight paperback copies of the works to be discussed for each session. According to Bullard, the eight, supplemented by additional copies requested through interlibrary loan, are "kept hidden" from the general public.

"Members of the reading group know to ask," Bullard says. "The neat part is that if twenty people come to talk about the book, twice that number from our fifty-person mailing list will have read it, as well. That underground movement is a pleasant thing for us."

Unlike most groups, the Saratoga Springs readers meet on no set day of no set week every month, so that the "free and open to the public" program accommodates a variety of schedules. During a summer session, a low attendance of five people was marked. *Song of Solomon* attracts forty, a record number of readers.

Among the forty are two teachers and a dozen students from Saratoga High School's AP English class, who had recently completed a unit on the book.

"I'd been trying to attract them since the group began meeting," Bullard says. "And this wasn't an assignment—attendance was only suggested."

The students and their teachers contribute much to the group's exploration of *Song of Solomon*, finding connections and meanings that hadn't surfaced in class work, asking questions, being excited. As it happens, the group's interpretations break along the contradictory lines that I'd found in reviews and scholarship, a testimony to the complexity of the novel. I ask question after question. The atmosphere is electric. The projected hour and a half session—7:30 to 9:00—stretches to two and a half hours. The juice, coffee, and cookies go untouched.

"Having writers in our midst not only allows the library to support them with exposure and money, but really enhances the group's experience, giving us new ways to think about what we read," Bullard says. "'I never thought of that' is not an unusual comment for us to hear."

For me, there is the opportunity to show how important reading is to a writer, that the answer to "where does a writer get ideas" is: everywhere. I'm also given a chance to show how one writer can stimulate another, how on a subconscious level, a writer might store an idea, bringing it to the surface much later, adapting it to the needs of a work, reexpressing it in his or her idiom.

I read my own story from the literary magazine in which it was published that summer, a story that in 1987 Morrison had especially liked. In "The Present," I used a device to explore the nature of memory while telling the story of giving a gift. In *Jazz*, Morrison also uses the device—a few pages in one chapter to show a character's feelings about herself. Moreover, the brief reading of that section of *Jazz* serves as introduction to the literary genres that, in *Song of Solomon*, Morrison transforms with both serious and humorous intent. "A writer," I tell them has been said, "is someone on whom nothing is ever lost."

While, like *Song of Solomon*, most books discussed are novels, the group has read plays, short story collections, narrative poetry, and some nonfiction. Writers' interests sometimes make for unusual, even difficult, selections. Popularity is not the key. A college instructor teaching himself to write creative essays chose *In Limestone Country* by Scott Russell Sanders, an example, he said, of the kind of work he wants to produce.

"It's a beautifully written book," says Bullard, who's not one to interfere with the writer's choice of book as long as she can buy paperback copies. "But not the sort of thing you'd expect a reading group to do. It's all about . . . well . . . limestone."

Whether the topic is limestone or, as has also been the case, lost fathers, the format of the Saratoga Springs Public Library reading group allows writers and readers to touch each other directly, an intimacy, a psychological connection that changes the relationship for both.

"Thank you," person after person stops to say to me, most touching my shoulder or arm, as they leave. And not only do I have my check in hand when I leave, but two days later, I receive a thank-you letter from Bullard. "Top notch," she writes. This woman knows how to treat a guest.

Success aside, Bullard thinks again of changing the way the program is run. "Summer is brutal," she says, referring to low attendance. "A writer who studied with him wants to review a novel by William Kennedy [*the* local writing celebrity], which should draw an audience, but otherwise I'd prefer to forget summer. There are so many other things going on here, including writing conferences with star readers. And before I burn out, I think I want to find someone who'll organize meetings and help select presenters, and do publicity. I don't want to let the series go. I'll reread my collection of resumes. I'll find someone."

SOMEONE HAS TO CARE ABOUT KIERKEGAARD

Stephanie Patterson
Philadelphia, Pennsylvania

S everal years ago I sat in a cafe with a friend. "The people I work with think Kierkegaard is a comic strip character," she complained. "If I mention John Donne, they want to know what kind of rock music he plays."

Sarah, fifteen years younger than I, was experiencing the post-academic depression that often envelops people when they discover that the intensity of the intellectual life they thrived on in college may have no counterpart in the world of work and marriage and children.

Her complaints resonated for me. I still read widely, but rarely discussed what I was reading beyond recommending a particular book. I spent years pursuing a Ph.D. in English Literature, but even in graduate school, discussions were more about receiving opinions from professors than listening to the fresher, if somewhat tentative, interpretations of my fellow students. Academia, in large measure, seemed to be made up of people talking to themselves.

Some months after my conversation with Sarah, a friend approached me about joining a book group. "We're doing Carl Sagan's *Cosmos*," said Linda. My heart did not flutter.

"What else is on the list?"

"*The First Salute.* You know, Barbara Tuchman's book."

"Don't you guys believe in fiction?"

"I'll get back to you."

While waiting for an answer, I began to slog through *The First Salute.* Not since my days of being frogmarched through James Fenimore Cooper had my favorite activity been so painful.

"Nobody in the group reads fiction," Linda reported a few days later.

"What?"

"Life's too short to spend time on things that aren't true." Thus ended my first attempt to join a book group.

A few months later I stood in line at a movie theater and listened to some older men and women discuss their Great Books group. As I joined the conversation, one gentleman, in his mid-sixties, eyed me hopefully. "Are you young? I'm looking for young people."

I hesitated. Men over the age of forty might feel a woman's youth ends at twenty-two, but this was book group, not a date, right?

"Yeah, I'm young." (I was thirty-seven at the time.)

This group was perfectly charming and welcoming and firmly established. But as the name Great Books suggests, most of their titles seemed to be selected from the canon of classics written by highly revered white men. While I admire ancient Greeks (Plato) and educated Virginians (Thomas Jefferson), I knew I wanted more say in what I read and what issues would be discussed.

Still, it was with some trepidation that I listened to my friend Kathy discuss her ideas about book groups. Thankfully, clichés sometimes do hold true—the third time was the charm.

Kathy had been part of a group that reads women authors. That particular group was time limited and Kathy and one of the other group members wanted to continue to meet. Each of them set out to recruit readers.

Seven people gathered for our first meeting. Though our group has now been together for three years and three of our original members have left, certain principles still apply. Including close friends in the group can help ensure that people feel a greater commitment to the initial undertaking (like Woody Allen said, half of life is showing up, and this is no-where truer than in a book group). But including people you don't know well socially—perhaps don't see outside the book group—reduces the risk that the group will metamorphose into a tony coffee klatch. The books our group chooses always have some claim to literary merit—no discussion of furniture and accessories in the fiction of Danielle Steele allowed. Our group also benefits from the wisdom of several generations. Fifty-year-old Susan can talk about how much *The Golden Notebook* meant to her when it was first published; twenty-nine-year-old Amy, for whom many of the accomplishments of the women's movement are faits accompli, brings a different perspective.

Our group has employed several methods of book selection. The group as originally advertised was to be devoted to the work of women authors. I came to the first meeting armed with an annotated syllabus.

"Wouldn't it be interesting," I asked, "to read Maxine Hong Kingston's *Woman Warrior*, Maya Angelou's *I Know Why the Caged Bird Sings*, and Annie Dillard's *An American Childhood* and compare the early experiences of three very different American women?"

"No," said Beverly, who taught English to teenage boys at a local Catholic prep school. "I refuse to read only women writers. It's too restrictive." Kathy and Amy both added they had read each of those books and had no interest in rereading them.

So we went on to discuss possible titles and different genres. Should we read plays occasionally? Did people prefer fiction or nonfiction? What writers should we read from other centuries and other cultures? Only one inviolable rule emerged from all this discussion.

"I'd like to read *Emma*," I said. "Jane Austen is so smart about women's roles in the nineteenth century."

"No Jane Austen," insisted Kathy, a woman whom I had always thought of as a person of taste and discernment.

"But I can even remember the first line of *Emma*," I persisted. "'Emma Woodhouse, handsome, clever, and rich . . .'"

"No Jane Austen."

"Those are adjectives usually applied to men. Don't you think that's worth discussing?"

"No."

"We could talk about how Emma makes trouble among her friends because she's not allowed to exert power in a larger society."

"No Jane Austen."

She won. I read Jane on the side—in solitary splendor.

After some lively debates during that initial meeting, we agreed on titles for our first few meetings: Isabel Allende's *Eva Luna*, Jane Rule's *Memory Board*, and Margaret Atwood's *Cat's Eye*. (Beverly was opposed to a group devoted solely to women's literature, not to one that emphasized it.)

Our meetings have never adhered to rigid format. Generally, one person is responsible for providing background on the author and the work. For newer authors, this may be a matter of reading interviews and reviews. When the group is reading a more established work, it is interesting to see how one's contemporary reading varies from generally accepted opinion.

Eva Luna was a major disappointment, especially to those in the group who had read *The House of the Spirits*. We wondered if Ms. Allende had lost interest in the work at some point and then rushed to finish the book.

Memory Board was admired because it dealt with people and issues often ignored in fiction. The protagonists are elderly and the conflict involves a man who is trying to make peace with his lesbian sister and her lover (who is suffering from Alzheimer's disease). Our reservations about the book lay in the feeling that the brother and sister were too easily reconciled and that the author, in an attempt to reach a mainstream audience, had made her gay characters flawless—and lifeless.

But the book did allow us to define certain issues and to maintain a sustained discussion about them.

The discussion of *Cat's Eye* was the defining moment for us. The story of Elaine's torment at the hands of her friend, Cordelia, struck a chord with all the members of our group. We discussed not only the book, but also our own struggles with classmates we had admired and feared. We were clearly a group of Elaines. Even now when friends inquire about our group, we suggest they read *Cat's Eye* and tell us with which character they identify. But we're not really sure Cordelias join book groups.

It was after the group had been meeting for about a year and a half that we lost several members to graduate school and new careers. We recruited new members from among our acquaintances. This change brought us our youngest and oldest members and a different emphasis in both book selection and discussion. We decided to read books that are denser in language, structure, and thought—books that required a sort of intellectual support group.

For example, to unravel the strands of consciousness that are woven together in Faulkner's *The Sound and the Fury*, each person, in addition to finishing the novel, was assigned the task of explaining a particular character and his function. Several readers were assigned to Benjy, some to Quentin, and one person kept track of chronology. The discussion extended to two sessions.

We also tackled *A Message to the Planet*, one of Iris Murdoch's philosophical treatises clothed as fiction. The discussion was not as lively as we had hoped because we became overwhelmed by the number of issues raised and the number of characters we had to keep straight.

But memories are short and the experience with Murdoch did not keep us from reading *War and Peace*. We found it wasn't so difficult to keep characters straight when they leapt fully realized from the page and did more than serve as mouthpieces for particular points of view. *Benet's Reader's Encyclopedia* provided good short treatments of both the Napoleonic Wars and Tolstoy's attitude toward various characters in the novel.

Though our group does not impose the same catechism of questions on each book, we have found that "So, did you like the book?" can be a real conversation stopper. If this question becomes the cornerstone of discussion, group members can get in the habit of neglecting to think beyond that point. The best discussions arise when readers have sharply differing views about the merits of a particular book and are forced to defend their opinions (the Sheltering Sky is a case in point).

Still, after three years, our group faced a mid-life crisis. We valued each others' companionship, but some of the thrill was gone. We devised a plan that we hoped would solve this problem, deciding to experiment, on occasion, with a new format where the group will have a theme, but we will not all be reading the same book.

Our initial attempt was a success. For a Yuletide meeting, each group member was asked to discuss five books that had influenced her as a child. Some of us were surprised to discover that many of our heroines were orphans (*Anne of Green Gables, Heidi, The House of Arden, A Little Princess, The Secret Garden*) or were raised by single parents (Nancy Drew, the five little Peppers). We were delighted that girls in these books were more adventurous than boys, but when we spoke to male friends, we discovered that they had been reading Robert Louis Stevenson and Joseph Conrad, writers who created worlds so devoid of women that, reading them, you wonder how the human race ever got perpetuated.

Our next experiment with this format will take place as the group focuses on John Kennedy. The creation and revision of the Kennedy myth started with the post-assassination memoirs (*The Pleasure of His Company*) and studies (*Death of a President*) and continues today in *J.F.K.: Reckless Youth*. The members of our group include some for whom the Kennedy administration was a vivid part of life and some for whom it is history. Bringing multiple historical and personal perspectives to a single figure may give us new understanding about our past and help us define what portions of the Kennedy legacy Bill Clinton might want to revisit during his administration.

While the members of this group may differ about what we should read and how we should approach various ideas, as long as we agree that books and the ideas in them are important, we'll continue to thrive. After all, someone has to care about Kierkegaard.

Exploring
Ourselves in
Surprising Ways

Martha Sloan
Deerfield, Illinois

Running a book discussion in a public library is a wonderful experience. People from vastly different backgrounds and age groups attend because they love books. All of us benefit as a result. The composition of our group eliminates the scourge of book groups made up of friends or neighbors—gossip—which so often leads the discussion away from the book. We are freer instead to concentrate only on the book we've all read.

The Deerfield Public Library serves a small community on Chicago's North Shore, where book groups are abundant. Also, many professional book group leaders and reviewers work in the area, leading discussions or giving lectures to private groups, clubs, and other libraries. The Deerfield Library group, however, is not formally run. As the Readers Services librarian, I usually lead the discussion. Occasionally the library director or another member helps out. During the past two years, a core group of women, and a few men, have attended faithfully, while others come and go. The average number of attendees is twenty-five, a little big. We discuss fiction and nonfiction.

The group started when I came to the library in 1991. I had no idea how to get the general public interested in coming to a library-sponsored book discussion. But because I enjoy memoirs and have found them to be of universal appeal, I advertised a discussion, stating that memoirs would be the topic. About twenty people attended that first meeting, and some have remained loyal members. Since that first meeting, we usually have discussed just one book. The library either buys paperbacks (I always choose books that are at least a year old) or gets copies from other libraries through interlibrary loan. I know of other libraries that offer books for sale to their discussion group members, but I have not yet done this.

Selecting books is one of the hardest decisions. I'm often surprised by what works for discussion and what doesn't. We do at least one classic a year. *Lady Chatterley's Lover* was the choice for Valentine's Day one year. None of the members had read it for years, if ever, and the poignancy of the romance contrasted with the dreariness of Lady Chatterley's marriage found new appeal to this group of mostly older readers. The group enjoys reading books they haven't read since youth and finding new meanings with their changed perspectives. *Emma* was another book we read with more mature eyes.

Our library director brings a different perspective. This past fall he dressed in his camping shorts, packed his backpack, pitched his tent, and led a lively discussion on one of his favorite books, Colin Fletcher's *The Man Who Walked Through Time*. His choice of the very bloody and militaristic *Son of the Morning Star* by Evan Connell drew a few more men than usual, but was not a success for the majority of the group. The battles and logistics were too detailed for most readers.

Although I serve coffee, the group is not social in its intent. However, in July we do something different. I select a genre, give out a list of suggested readings, and ask the group to read one book or another of his or her choice and be prepared to share it. Victorian mysteries and favorite romances are two themes we've had. This format gives me a break and is a chance for light summer reading.

Lately, we have been reading new authors or first novels. Barbara Kingsolver's *The Bean Trees* was an instant success. We explored the different family relationships, her sense of humor, her warmth, and her optimism—a great choice for the Christmas season. *The Music Room* by Dennis McFarland was not so universally loved. It is a story of a truly unhappy family, suicide, and self-discovery. However, as one woman stated, "It resonates. It doesn't let you go." Less successful, but most interesting for me, was the selection of Alice Munro's short stories from *A Friend of My Youth*. Attendance reached a low point, yet there was so much to discuss and explore that I could barely get through two stories. Though the group wasn't enthusiastic, I will try short stories again. I haven't yet done any poetry, partly because I'm not confident of my own knowledge in this area.

Because I believe that books are a way for us to touch each other and explore ourselves in surprising ways, this rather diverse book discussion group has formed a life of its own. People feel free to share family secrets and personal longings. In a strange way books provide the safety of distance, but also are an avenue to our more real selves.

I try to walk a fine line between discussing personal incidents and the book. Only rarely does someone stray too far off the subject. *From Beirut to Jerusalem* attracted many one-time attendees and led to vociferous opinions. I had to remain in complete control. However, I usually can allow some deviation from the text without destroying the flow of the discussion. In addition, I try to introduce some understanding of the construction of the novel and the author's technique and language, which may elude the reader. I also share other reviewers' points of view and offer some background on the author. The members appreciate this insight. As a former teacher, I construct the hour and a half as I would a class. Even though I do not hold myself or the group to my "lesson plan," I have found that the structure gives me a sense of what I want to cover and a framework for the time period.

I firmly believe that holding book discussions is an integral part of the role of a public library. I see one of our basic functions as reaching out to the community, sharing good books, and introducing readers to new authors and new ideas. Book discussions are also a wonderful way to build good will and enthusiasm for the library. Any library has a few loyal readers who could be asked to form the core of a group, and once a group has begun, participants will follow.

EVERY WOMAN HAS A STORY

Janet Tripp
Minneapolis, Minnesota

For the past thirteen years, my book group has been a signpost for my life. It points me in new directions. It shores me up and remains my constant in a world of flux. Regardless of what is happening around us, on the second Friday morning of every month, our circle of fifteen women gathers. What began in 1980 as six sessions of a university literature class in women's autobiography has continued over the years, becoming an integral part of all our lives.

Jeanette and Dory are retired and travel. Their departures and arrivals revolve around the second Friday of the month. Margie and Rachel are newly graduated young professionals whose full-time work requires plausible excuses for their absence each second Friday. Maddy has a new baby and Libby visiting grandchildren that must be provided for so that on the second Friday of every month we can gather to discuss the current book on our reading list.

Every six months we select six new titles and recommit ourselves by writing a check for our leader, Toni McNaron, the English professor whose class was the nucleus of the group. Toni requires four things of the selection process. We read only books by women, at least one poet, some work by women of color, and one selection of an earlier time. We sit in a circle balancing a cup of coffee or tea and bagel, muffin, or stollen, and begin promptly. In the first lap around the circle, each woman defines what the book means to her. What she feels, wonders, thinks, rejects, and is moved by. We listen and she speaks uninterrupted, often reading aloud favorite passages that relate the book's import to her life. After that, we have a general discussion and Toni offers biographical comments or literary history. We conclude by sharing our own writing with the group.

Our goal is to read our own work to the group every other month. Most of us do not think of ourselves as writers, but we read memoirs written for our children and grandchildren, letters to the editor, essays, short stories, journal entries, letters to friends, poetry—and occasionally even a published piece. Often the reader's voice will quiver with nervousness and with the emotions stirred up by the words.

I do not see most of these women for the rest of the month, but what we share in that two-hour period creates a circle of fire that energizes me for days. We have no name, but I think of us as Toni's Group—her direction and intellect provide our focus. She tells us of the feminist theory that every woman has a story. She presents the scope of women's realities, creating "a forum in which more and more women can get out more and more parts of their stories. We have such a forum in this group," she tells us, "and this may be its most precious aspect."

Our experience with the book often extends beyond the printed page. We have invited authors to our meetings to answer questions and respond to our discussion. Madelon Sprengnether, Paulette Bates Alden, Phoebe Hansen, and Grace Paley have met with us. We have sat in the audience to hear Audre Lorde, Tillie Olsen, Maxine Hong Kingston, Lorene Cary, Leslie Marmon Silko, and Adrienne Rich. After reading *Out of Africa*, we saw the movie together. Inspired by our reading, we self-published a collection of our writing. We have been interviewed on a local public radio talk show, and hosted a book signing for the publication of Toni's memoir, *I Dwell in Possibility*.

I have been changed by this circle of women. In 1980, when we began as a class, I disliked the autobiographical genre, but over the years I have grown to prefer real life stories—autobiography, biography, and nonfiction memoir. They help me live my life, often serving as a model for coping. They place problems in perspective and in history, and they show me that living one's life can be one's art.

Over time our group has changed. After her husband died, Ruth retired and moved to Yemen with the Peace Corps. In the beginning, our oldest member, Helmi, attended with her daughter. She told us about reading what we now consider classics in their original printing—of the importance to her of the "new" work by Katherine Mansfield, M. F. K. Fisher, and Willa Cather. Now Helmi is in a nursing home, but her granddaughter has joined us, allowing the group to remain multigenerational.

We are together still because of our focus. Toni propels us forward with her structure and vision. She tells us over and over again, "women's words are valuable." She empowers us by insisting we write. We acknowledge each others' words by listening. Together we read books that individually we'd never have chosen. We write words that would have been left unsaid.

Sometimes there are surprises. I come to group hating a book, only to hear wonderful passages read out loud and someone's appreciation for it based on her perspective. We are Jew, Christian, and Pagan, married and not, wealthy and struggling, lesbian and heterosexual. What others bring to a book is often entirely different from my own familiar baggage. In the exchanges, I have learned to be critical in my reading, to question who is profiting in a situation, to appreciate what a painful, unfamiliar, antagonistic story can offer. I have learned to call these women, different from myself, "friend."

Of the 156 books we have read, some caused such lively discussion or created such indelible impressions that they stand out in my mind. I think of *Storyteller* by Leslie Marmon

Silko—of her exploration of form, and the best short story I have ever read. Jamaica Kincaid's *Annie John*, with its richness and depth, moved me to see memoirs in a new way and to try my hand at the form. *Revelations: Diaries of Women*, edited by Mary Jane Moffat and Charlotte Painter, was the diving-off place for our years of exploration together. The trilogy *Kristin Lavransdatter* by Sigrid Undset moved me into another time like no other book has done. Tsitsi Dangarembga's story *Nervous Conditions* brought home to me the devastating repression of being female and colonized.

The books are the connection, but the heart of the group, the fire that draws me back again and again, is the circle of women, their acceptance of my ideas, and questions about my reading. It is a place to come home to. I want to hear what these women think and what they are writing. The texts we read and the written words of the group show me what women can do, how powerful we can be, how good we are.

THURSDAY EVENINGS

Susan Knoppow
Royal Oak, Michigan

When I was growing up, I knew a few things for certain: my sister Ellen was a better fighter than me; "Underdog" came on TV at lunchtime; and book club met the first Thursday of every month.

As the years went on, Ellen and I gave up fighting with our fists and feet, and I started packing my lunch to eat in the school cafeteria. But today, twenty-seven years after they started it as a way to get out of the house and away from husbands and new babies, my mom and her oldest friends still meet on first Thursdays at 8:00 to talk about the books they read.

The book club ladies rotate houses and take turns "doing the book," which means going to the library and finding out as much as possible about the book and its author. They make xerox copies and coffee. There are about fifteen of them—women in their early fifties who have known each other since high school, plus various friends they've accumulated over the years. Mrs. Lieberman has been a member for less than fifteen years. I still think of her as "new."

Husbands disappear on these nights. There is always cake. As children, Ellen and I would take plates of dessert upstairs where we watched TV in our pajamas. We stretched out on our parents' bed and drank milk. Sometimes we'd sneak downstairs for another snack, slipping past the ladies in the living room, embarrassed and pleased to be noticed.

As I got older, I began reading the books too. Sylvia Plath and Charles Dickens. Michael Dorris and Ellen Gilchrist. Mostly fiction. Mostly novels. Books were something my mother and I shared.

When I graduated from college and moved back to Detroit, most of my friends were gone. For all intents and purposes, I was new in town. The streets were familiar, but the people were not. I needed a book club of my own. But how to find one?

I began by calling bookstores and libraries. No luck. Libraries had occasional lectures or discussion groups at noon, but I had to work during the day. Bookstore clerks found my inquiry interesting, but they couldn't help me either.

Then I noticed an ad in the local alternative newspaper. "Feminist Reading Group," it said, "Call Shirley." So I did.

Shirley was surprised to hear from me. The ad was supposed to have been pulled three months before, she told me, but somehow it kept popping up. "This month we're reading *Cat's Eye* by Margaret Atwood. You're welcome to join us. We meet the second Thursday."

On the second Thursday in August, I knocked on Pam's door. I was not so sure anymore. A book club was something I associated with old friends who'd bought their first pantyhose together—women who'd watched each others' children head off to kindergarten and college. It was not a place to be on a stranger's doorstep with a copy of *Cat's Eye* under your arm and a stomach in knots.

That first meeting I sat very quietly on the couch. I watched and listened. They seemed to forget I was there. The second and third times I went were a little better, but I couldn't quite get the names straight. And how did they all know each other, anyway? Every month I showed up at this mysterious and friendly club, but no one took the time to find out who I was or why I was there.

It wasn't until about six months later that I felt as if I belonged. By then I was something of a regular and I had pieced together the group's history, which went something like this. Around 1986, a group of women decided to start a reading group. They had husbands and children and jobs, and they liked books. They decided that the reading group would stick to books written by women—they all read enough books written by men anyway. This group would be different.

Over the years, the group evolved. Some members moved away. Others became busy with obligations and floated in and out. People invited their friends. Some of us are friends outside the group; others are not. Some of us have jobs outside the home; others do not. We're single, married, divorced, widowed, mothers, grandmothers. We argue over the merits of science fiction and short stories.

Our group has traditions. We have a summer potluck at Shirley's in June, where we drink wine and sit on her patio. We're informal—no assigned dishes—one year everyone brought pasta salad.

Around Christmastime we gather for dinner at Pam's. This time we're more formal. We get the good china and silver. Pam builds a fire in the fireplace and plays jazz on the stereo.

February is poetry. Everyone brings copies of a favorite poem. Sometimes we bring pieces we've written ourselves. We generally tackle one heavy-duty nonfiction book a year. Something scholarly and important that takes us three or four months to finish. We try to stay away from hardcovers. They're tempting, but expensive.

My book club is different from my mother's. Our members are all ages. We're more transient. We don't usually feed each other. It's an extremely intimate group, though many of us hardly know each other. We talk about everything, most of which has very little to do with the books we read. Every so often we make a rule about really discussing the book, but then we break it. Mostly, we like each others' company.

POLICIES FOR
LADIES WHO READ

Marilyn Monaco-Han
Brooklyn, New York

The consensus of our group, seven people whom I will describe later, is that every group must have a policy if they are to have any chance at longevity and harmony. We realized this only after some pain, but then everyone in our group agrees that the pain was a symptom, probably an unavoidable one, for any group that begins informally and whose main reason for being is that the members love books and yearn to share that passion with similar-minded people.

Our group began in 1987 when a few college students of advanced age remarked that they would like to continue reading in a structured way and discussing books with their Professor. The Professor agreed that an informal setting where she would simply be another member of the discussion group was also to her liking. The students then recruited friends or acquaintances who they knew liked to read.

The group began with no rules. As might have been expected, the Professor took the lead and directed the choice of reading with some input from the group, organized the discussion, often giving biographical background on the author or the period in which the book was written, and generally guided the discussion of the book in a manner similar to that used in a classroom.

Those members from the original class continued to express their enthusiasm for the Professor's leadership, but then an odd thing happened. The Professor was a cerebral, cool, motherly type who reigned without challenge until another member invited a woman who was an earthy, emotive, motherly type. The two mothers instantly disliked each other. Whenever earth mother spoke, cerebral mother took a deep breath and then disagreed or contradicted or simply ignored her. The tension between the two was nearly palpable and unrelenting. Cerebral mother began to miss sessions, offering flimsy excuses.

Finally, one of the members called the Professor and asked what was going on. The Professor said she simply could not stand to attend knowing the other woman would be there. This member decided that the only solution was to disinvite earth mother, who apparently was tremendously relieved to be rid of the obligation. The crisis nearly broke up the group. Everyone was glad when earth mother left—not because she wasn't liked—but because the Professor was thought to be too valuable a participant to lose, and the crisis had been exhausting. And so the group survived, though its tenor was a bit different, and the Professor played a less commanding role.

Still, it was felt she gave more than she got. But then an incident occurred that made it clear that the group was perhaps more important to the Professor than anyone had realized. It happened one night when the group met during a great storm. They could hear the rain coming down in proverbial buckets. People seemed stalled indoors. The Professor got up to leave first, announcing that she was unprepared for the great storm. One member kindly lent her an umbrella. The Professor still hesitated—perhaps she needed a rain slicker. Fine. Another member produced a slicker. Then came the request for boots and a hat, both of which were magically produced.

Finally, she was ready to brave the elements. The group watched her depart, and then heard three hurried steps against the pavement, a car door slamming, and a motor starting. The Professor's car was parked mere yards from the front door. The group burst into laughter, but this scenario helped the members realize that they indeed had something to give the Professor. The group was not a one-way street.

This story also points to an important point about any group—it should be as close to a democracy as possible. It should exist in an atmosphere where the members understand that though members with strong personalities might dominate the discussion, everyone is free and welcome to express an opinion.

The Professor eventually left the group for reasons unrelated to the earth mother crisis. She did not leave cleanly though. She simply failed to come to any meetings for a three- or four-month period during which the group went on in the atmosphere of "Waiting for Godot." One current member, who joined the group at that time, recalls how strange it was that each meeting had this aura of what the Professor might say or do. Once it was certain the Professor wouldn't return, the group promptly began to formulate its policy, which we've followed since.

The policy was written and then circulated among members for discussion and editing. It is entitled simply, "Policies for Ladies Who Read." It has seven points: 1) We are a group of ladies who gather monthly to discuss a book that we have chosen to read (I should add here that when I asked the group whether they had made a conscious decision to invite only women, they answered that they had never intended to be inclusive, and that was that). 2) We are social from approximately 7:00 to 7:30. If there are newcomers, they are introduced and welcomed during this time. 3) After 7:30, the person previously designated as the month's leader takes charge of the discussion. At this time, newcomers are told of the two- meeting trial period during which we all see how we relate to one another and to the purpose of the group as a whole. Each newcomer is given a copy of our policy sheet, a list of books previously read, and a contact sheet of current members. The policies are read aloud. 4) The current leader then starts our formal discussion of the book we've read for the meeting. The time should be 8:00. 5) We assume each member has read the book. If they have not because they hated it or it was impossible to do so, they tell us why they felt this way. They also may choose not to participate in the discussion. 6) Once we finally begin the formal discussion, the leader's responsibility is to keep us from digressing—to make sure we have a thorough discussion, exhausting all of our individual insights, opinions, thoughts, and feelings about the book and the author. If we do digress or become too social, the leader should gently bring us back to our purpose. 7) Finally, the next meeting's leader shows or tells us about the books from which we will choose the next month's selection. The choice is by majority vote. Then a request is made for a volunteer to bring books to the next meeting. We choose a date and site for the next meeting, accommodating everyone's schedule.

This simple policy has worked well with our group—we address particular problems as they arise. For instance, we have from time to time explored the idea of venturing outside the realm of fiction, but no one has really pushed the idea of an alternative genre. No doubt the group will someday branch out to plays or biography or feminist thought, but this hasn't happened yet.

As I said before, there are seven of us, a number we all agree is nearly perfect for a good discussion. We meet in New York City, although only one of us is a native New Yorker. Two of our members are actresses who also have jobs outside the theater. One of the actresses works at Carnegie Hall in administration. It was here that she met one of the original members of the group who invited her to join our book group. Two other members are college students who are completing degrees after being away from school for a time. One member is the owner and manager of a liquor store, having previously been a wine salesperson and a bookseller. The last member is a disaffected lawyer.

As a group, we have no unifying threads other than our love of books and cats and the ability to read quickly and never lose interest in all variety of good writing. Invariably during our social time we talk about movies and plays and sometimes politics, though this is not a favorite topic, just sometimes a pressing one. We also keep abreast of each others' work and travels.

Our group is experienced enough to appreciate a bit of formality, especially during a discussion when somebody thinks of herself as more interesting than any fiction. We gently and firmly bring the discussion back to the book, without being so controlling that we insult the principle of free expression. While cohesion is difficult to build and maintain, fresh blood is an asset, so we do invite new members from time to time.

With respect to the selection of books, we have no formal guidelines. We choose from whatever the next month's leader presents. Of course, everyone wants to please, so some thought is given to the tastes of the group. We try to keep in mind that the book should be discussable. This may sound like an ephemeral quality, but if you have had some experience in a group or classroom, you'll realize that many otherwise fine books are difficult to talk about. For example, though we loved *To Kill a Mockingbird*, our group had little to say about it.

Loving a book may in fact be the death knell for discussion. We have found that often the books we liked least provoked the best discussion. Controversy also breeds lively discussion, so we don't shrink from disagreement. We also try to vary the type of book or subject matter. If we have just read two books full of domestic tragedy, we schedule something more cerebral or historical.

We usually have a fair amount of variety, not concentrating on female authors, though they are well represented, or modern novels as opposed to classics. We did once feel so strongly positive about a book, *Aquamarine* by Carol Anshaw, that we sent a letter of appreciation to the author. Ms. Anshaw wrote back, which delighted us and made us aware of a small, mutual admiration society between a working author and an unknown reading group.

We have nothing but kind words of encouragement for any beginning or struggling reading group. It can be done, and so you must do it and make it whatever you desire, but you *must* have a policy.

INITIATION
RITES

Susanna Tull
Toronto, Ontario, Canada

In my Christmas stocking this year my husband (jokingly, I hope) tucked a copy of a little book titled *Books Are Better in Bed Than Men Because. . . .* This gift brought into focus just how important my books and my book groups are to me.

Books have always been an essential part of my life, delightfully occupying many an idle vacation hour and helping me through many other bored, sick, or lonely moments. Joining my first book group four and a half years ago in Seattle was like finding soulmates—I'd finally discovered a support group for biblioholics. I relished our monthly meetings and annual retreats as opportunities to enjoy the company of remarkable women and excellent books.

Book groups fulfill many functions. They provide those of us home with small children an opportunity not to feel braindead one evening a month. The meetings give members something to talk about *other* than their children. They also are great for making new friends and socializing. But, most important, they encourage the exchange of ideas and book titles and require members (all of who think they have zero free time) to read at least one book a month.

In each of the three book groups in which I've participated (I've moved from Seattle to Toronto where I've joined one book group and started another), the general format has been similar. We meet once a month in a member's home to discuss a previously agreed-upon book. Whichever member has volunteered her home provides refreshments.

Usually a member has done some advance research on the book such as gathering reviews and biographical information about the author, and she begins the discussion by sharing her findings. This background information frequently generates a lively discussion. Do the members agree with the reviewers? What are the main themes of the book? How has the writer's background come to bear on the work? These questions become points of departure.

Part of what makes a book group stimulating is the sunburst of tangential directions our discussions often take. We might debate the merits of a particular book for forty-five minutes or we might talk about the selected book for ten minutes and end up using it as a springboard for a discussion of sex, politics, public education, or some other indirectly related theme. Because of the informal structure of the group, the discussion goes where the whim of the group and the idiosyncrasies of its members take it.

Along with the discussion of the book of the month comes a terrific exchange of other titles and authors. I always bring a notepad along to jot down the other members' latest literary discoveries. We then either collectively agree upon the next book (sometimes we plan the next two or three months' reading), or, if there is no consensus, whoever is hosting next selects the book. The meeting winds down with refreshments and socializing. Depending on the mood of the group and the liveliness of the discussion, a meeting typically runs about three hours.

The decision to meet at night or during the day affects both the group's composition and the tone of the meetings. Evening groups tend to be more relaxed—a glass of wine often loosens the mind and the tongue. The morning group's discussion stays more focused on the book and is often more literary in nature. Scheduling depends, of course, on what members want and what type of members the group wants. An evening group can include a more diverse membership as it doesn't automatically exclude those who work outside the home.

The books chosen are also a reflection of the membership's expectations about the purpose of the group. My evening group consists of women who love to read but don't have a whole lot of time to do so and mostly want a night out with their women friends. As a result, we primarily read current fiction. We keep debating whether to pick a theme for the year's reading. After a wild discussion of Anne Rice's *Cry to Heaven*, the group agreed that sex would be a good theme for 1993.

In contrast, my morning book group takes its reading quite seriously. It's associated with the Toronto Newcomers Organization and is composed of women from all over the world. The group tends to read classics (perfect for those of us who missed them in our youth) and international authors and has provided me with wonderful suggestions of authors and titles that were previously unfamiliar to me. However different, both groups are characterized by good conversation, a shared love of books, and developing friendships.

It's important and sometimes difficult to select books that lend themselves well to discussion. Once a group is up and rolling and the members know each others' tastes and interests, book selection by consensus comes more easily. Some books seem to be surefire discussion generators (a list of "best discussion" titles is included in the list section of this book). Another way for either a new or established group to select books is for each member to choose a book associated with an agreed-upon theme.

Even the most enduring groups will occasionally have trouble in paradise. Members' lives and schedules sometimes become too hectic and attendance falls, or people haven't read the book and the discussion suffers. To counter faltering attendance, it's useful to ask the hostess to call members the week before the meeting to remind and encourage them to attend. To combat lack of enthusiasm or group lethargy, potential new members should be encouraged to attend periodically and the group should do something a little different at a meeting. We once began a discussion of P. D. James's *A Taste for Death* by watching her PBS interview with Al Page. Another way to stir things up is to invite a guest speaker or to share personal "Top Ten" reading lists.

All three of the groups I've been involved in take a summer break in July and August. We do, however, send each other off with summer reading lists and try to decide on the September book when we meet in June. Additionally, we try to pick a relatively short book for December and make the December meeting more of a social event. In Seattle we each brought a wrapped, favorite paperback to the December meeting and put all the books on a table. We each took a book and un-wrapped it. We went around the room then one by one and each member was allowed to either keep the book she had or exchange the book with that of another member, whether that member wanted to make a trade or not.

This year in Toronto, one of my groups celebrated the holidays by lunching together at a nice restaurant, while the other group discussed Émile Zola's *Thérèse Raquin* and sampled Swedish, American, and Canadian holiday treats. In addition to being a lot of fun, these holiday variations help keep members enthused about the group.

Another way to keep interest high is to schedule periodic retreats or getaway weekends. In Seattle we picked a June weekend each year and as many of us as possible took off for such adventures as a weekend in a historic inn, two days of horseback riding at a dude ranch, or a luxury overnight in a downtown hotel suite. My fledgling Toronto group really likes the retreat idea and is planning a ski weekend and theater outing (we'll read *The Stone Angel* by Margaret Laurence and then see the stage version) in coming months. The only limit to creative options is the members' imaginations.

Book group night or morning each month has become something of a sacred event in my house. My children know that Mommy's book group is important stuff. When my son was seven years old, he offered to read aloud to the group—I think he thought it was some sort of initiation rite and he definitely wanted to join the club. Or perhaps he sees that for me book groups have provided new friends, a wealth of literary camaraderie, and the exquisite opportunity to share the love of reading with like-minded readers.

WHY ONLY BOOKS BY WOMEN?

Barbara Kerr Davis
Exeter, California

Recently, I caught just the end of a program on public television—a dramatization of the life of Ernest Hemingway. Even in those few minutes, the Hemingway I remember was there—boyhood hours of fishing, hunting, and visiting the Indians with his father, his wartime experience with the Red Cross, his philosophy of "destroyed but not defeated" from *The Old Man and the Sea*, his father's suicide—all the much admired masculine style and subject matter of the Code Hero. I'm not saying that I didn't enjoy reading Hemingway. It will be forever a part of my consciousness that "the earth moved" for Maria and Robert in *For Whom the Bell Tolls*, and I still am in awe of the Indian who killed himself in sympathy for the woman who was giving birth to his child.

No, reading male writers like Hemingway did not dissuade me from reading nor from enjoying what I read. In fact, I had always loved to read, and I hardly discerned between one author and another, only asking for a good story, an interesting setting, and a sympathetic character—male or female—to keep me reading. Through high school and college I read many of the "great" writers of English prose and poetry and was only vaguely aware that most of them were men—Shakespeare, Milton, Pope, Swift, Dickens, Tennyson, D. H. Lawrence. Oh, there were a few women; one gave herself a man's name (George Eliot), and there was Jane Austen who was limited, it was said, by her miniature society. And there was Virginia Woolf, the rather neurotic Englishwoman who wrote in an obscure, new style and later drowned herself.

In graduate school I found a few more women writers—Colette, Edith Wharton, Elizabeth Barrett Browning, and Iris Murdoch. But still, I accepted almost without question the canon of "great literature" as determined largely by males and consisting largely of male authors—James Joyce, Henry James, Robert Browning, William Faulkner, Charles Dickens, and E. M. Forster. I once took a seminar entitled "The Two Georges" meaning George Meredith and George Eliot, and in my still relatively unconscious state I chose to write my dissertation on the man, George Meredith.

But then, just near the end of my graduate school days, two other women students and I founded a reading group to read women writers. Our first book was Kate Chopin's *The Awakening*. I remember sitting with that group of women—all of us were students or teachers—and feeling that we were discovering a hidden treasure trove of real, good, even great literature by women. Where had those works been? Why had they been kept from us? Later, I had my first child, my daughter Lisa, whom I proudly brought to book club one night while she was a nursing infant, and I was determined: she wouldn't grow up thinking that only men had created the world's great art!

We read a great many women during those years despite our busy student and teaching schedules. Most of us were in our twenties—though we had a few older women as well—and women's studies courses were being instituted in some colleges; affirmative action was taking hold in our own university, and women were struggling to keep their sense of humor to balance the long-pent-up rage that was finally being expressed.

When I moved to San Diego—now mother to a year-old son, Peter, as well as three-year-old Lisa—a mention of my wish to begin a women's book group was immediately taken up by two friends, and in January of 1977 we began a group that grew and changed over the years but became a cohesive unit as we met in each others' homes every month. We read novels, short stories, mysteries, poetry, biographies, classics, foreign works—all by women. In sharing our ideas and feelings about what other women had written, we wove together the strands of our own lives, a "weave of women."

When the Providers sent me to the Northwest Zone (à la Lessing!), a graduate school friend gathered together a group of women, and we also met each month throughout the year to read books by women. After about a year, this group, too, found its core.

After the Northwest Zone (read Portland, Oregon), I moved with my family to Los Angeles for four years. I began yet another book group there, which met and read women writers each month. I believe that at least some of the same members continue in the group. When I moved to central California, to a rather small town, I joined a "Beyond War" group (for peace) that has now become a women's book group.

Last spring I visited my San Diego book group when they had a fifteenth-year celebration. We all contributed some written piece, which we read aloud to the group—a very moving experience. They continue to meet each month, alas, without me. But I still feel very close to them because of all we've shared.

Why read women? My experience in all these book groups indicates that women are eager to read the words, the thoughts, the memories, and the feelings of other women— about childbearing in medieval Norway, struggling in poverty in the Appalachians, being black in America, dealing with racial problems in South America, moving through zones of consciousness on an imaginary planet, or falling in love in modern London. We do not reject the old "greats" of male literature. Indeed, we need to understand male perceptions of the world as well. But it is certainly time that we recognize that there is much great and good literature by women as well.

THE RAD READING ZAPPERS

Molly Blake Leckie
Greenwich, Connecticut

The call came as we were sitting down for dinner one June evening. My daughter's fourth grade teacher spoke distinctly, "I'm so sorry to tell you that Catherine did not do well on her last reading test. Because of her scores, it will be necessary for her to change reading groups. Please explain the situation to her, and tell her to *read, read, read* over summer vacation."

Oh, how I hate those numbers that classify readers—advanced, average, remedial. Being an avid reader, I have trouble understanding how the school system rates appreciation of a good story. Still, reading does not come easily to my daughter, and the fun of a good story had been lost to her. Later that evening, I talked to Catherine about the phone message and tried to reassure her that all would work out. Her dark eyes flashed with discouragement and hurt as she blasted, "I hate to read, and I don't want to make reading a hobby like you do!" Tucking my active go-getter into bed, my advice not to worry sounded lame even to me.

A few days later, school drew to a close. Catherine and I brought a small gift to her teacher and picked up the book list for summer reading. While we were chatting, Catherine's friend Megan stopped to look at the list of books. "I hate to read," was her quick response to my inquiry about which book she would read first. Handing me the list, Catherine ran off with her to play, laughing as she commented, "Join the club!"

Driving home I thought about Catherine's comment. Maybe she was onto something. We could start a reading club for the summer. The more I thought about it, the more excited I became at the prospect of sharing my love of literature. If we combined my enthusiasm with their youthful imagination, the girls might begin to understand that there is more to reading than sitting in a chair and looking at the pages in a book. We could meet in the evenings. Approval from the other parents would solidify the plan.

After a phone call to Megan's mom and another friend, Kristi's mother, I stood armed with overwhelming support and encouragement. I approached the girls with the scheme and they thought it was a great idea. Young girls love to bond, unite, and group—a club that would meet once a week to discuss what they were reading and have refreshments certainly seemed worthwhile to them.

The first meeting found the four of us with notepads, pencils, and books gathered in the living room. We sat around the coffee table, which was laden with brownies, lemonade, and children's poetry books. My first concern was establishing two rules that I felt had to be enforced if the group was to work. First, respect for each other and their feelings. As the girls would say, NO Put Downs! If someone broke this rule, they would be excused from the meeting for that evening. The second rule was equally as important—competition would not be tolerated. We would lose respect for the literature if we began to worry about who read the most. We all had different reading abilities and the club was about sharing stories. The girls did not have a problem understanding and accepting the need for such controls. As Catherine pointed out, I could outread them all.

We were ready then to move on to the matter of a name for the group. The problem of hurt feelings was easily avoided as the club members decided to take one word from each girl's suggestion. The Rad Reading Zappers were officially ready to begin sharing tales and, of course, refreshments.

Each member, including me, took a turn describing the book she was reading, and let the rest of the group know if she would recommend it. I called this segment of the meeting reporting. After reading passages from their books and drinking lemonade, the girls took the poetry books and began reciting and acting out some of their favorite poems. This was dramatic and funny. Humorous poetry is easily the Rad Reading Zappers's number one choice. Before we knew it, the other girls' moms were pulling in the driveway and our first meeting ended. Megan summed up everyone's feelings as she left, "That was so much fun. Let's meet twice a week!"

As the summer progressed, so did the group. We met weekly to share our thoughts and homemade goodies and to work on projects. The girls made posters advertising their club and decorated the school library with them. If a member was away on vacation, she sent us a postcard and returned to our meeting with brochures and pamphlets describing where she'd been. For the missing member, the others tape-recorded poems, jokes, riddles, and excerpts from the books they were reading. Within a few weeks, Megan started collecting bookmarks, Kristi started a scrapbook, and Catherine was writing stories and plays for the girls to read and perform.

We also took a few field trips to the library. The girls browsed through the periodical section, searching for articles on subjects that interested them. They became adept in making copies from the microfilm and then sharing their newfound information. The reports ranged from endangered species to fashion models. Of course, each trip ended at the ice cream shop with the girls reciting the menu from memory.

As summer drew to a close, we decided the Rad Reading Zappers needed a gala finish, and we planned two events. The first was a poetry and play reading for members' families. Everyone brought desserts to add to the celebration. The girls' exuberance was contagious. It was an evening of families brought together by the pure enjoyment of reading.

The second event on the Rad Reading Zappers's calendar, which I agreed to in a moment of weakness, was a sleepover party. The girls planned a surprise presentation for me—they picked their favorite book from the summer reading list and dressed as one of the characters in it. After reading and pizza it was easy to settle them with a goodnight story.

The next morning over orange juice and muffins, the girls told me they wanted to continue the club during the school year if I was willing to participate. We discussed the feasibility in light of busy schedules and decided we would try to meet twice a month. Who could say no to three ten-year-old girls who wanted to read?

We started plotting plans for the year. We'd supplement their science and history courses by reading about famous people and attending meetings as that person. We talked about going to a day-care center and reading and acting out stories to younger children or visiting homebound elderly people and reading to them. The girls were bubbling with ideas and suggestions.

The Rad Reading Zappers's summer ended with an enthusiasm for reading that I never thought I would see when the group began. The girls developed discerning taste in literature, sharpened their analytical skills, and bolstered their confidence in presenting their thoughts. Without realizing what was taking place, the girls turned a negative into a positive experience. We all benefited by exchanging ideas, communicating our interest, and appreciating each other.

In retrospect, I can see there are a few reasons why the club was successful. We had no expectations of what would transpire. We simply followed our two rules—respect for each other and the literature—and watched as enthusiasm carried us through. I learned an important lesson too. When hanging around with kids, the best advice is to *listen, listen, listen.* If you do that, you'll be amazed at how much you'll learn.

TALKING AS QUILTING

Ellie Becker
Santa Fe, New Mexico

"Tomas is an arrogant creep. I hate him, and I don't like the book," declares Sharon. Thus begins the discussion of Milan Kundera's *Incredible Lightness of Being* and my initiation into book group. While no one embraces Tomas's point of view, some are more sympathetic than Sharon. Most of us admire Kundera's uncanny ability to get inside the heads of both man and woman. In our discussion, we touch on love, narcissism, monogamy, moral truth, political repression, compassion versus pity. Are all metaphors dangerous, as Tomas held, because "a single metaphor can give birth to love?"

At first, we take our predictable stances. Liz uses precise language, is careful and in control, an acute observer of the language and action of the characters. Sharon looks at dysfunction, right behavior, social justice. Lynn speaks directly, concerned with the sense and sensibleness of both the story and the characters. Leslie's meticulous reading unearths subtle phrases most of us have missed—she is soft-spoken, thorough, literal, and finds Tomas morally reprehensible. Jane listens

carefully, and examines unfamiliar points of view in a respect-
ful way. By the end of the discussion, we have experienced
some shift in perception. Our combined perspectives have
enriched our understanding of the book. We do not change
who we are, but we become more than we were.

The Kundera discussion took place five years ago, and we
have since sharpened our analytical skills. We are all women, a
core group of seven that has been together since 1988. Two
others participate on an irregular basis; two attended for about
a year and then left the group. The one common thread is that
we are all graduates of or tutors at St. John's College (this was
not a prerequisite for joining, however). The St. John's curric-
ulum is based on discussion of the Great Books, thus we were
instantly at ease talking about books.

We aren't best friends, although many friendships have
deepened, and we have come to know one another better.
There is always plenty to say before we start talking about the
book. We know by now that tea will be set out, along with
edibles of some sort.

We begin the discussion with a question—a real question,
not a rhetorical one. We stick to the text, only going off on
tangents that make sense in the context of the book. No one
comes for therapy or self-indulgence.

Still, it's more than talking about books, more than a seminar at St. John's. We share news and feelings about relationships, births, miscarriages, loss, joy, and sadness. We discuss
gender, a woman's power (and lack of), and moral choices.
These topics spring from the books themselves, yet they are
treated in a deeper-than-academic manner.

One book in particular, *A Midwife's Tale* by Martha Ballard,
generated discussion of what the group meant to us and the
function it performed in our lives. We spoke of the dearth of
opportunities for women—and men—to gather together for a
common purpose. *A Midwife's Tale* presents excerpts from the
diary of Martha Ballard (1785–1812). In Martha's time, people
could not be isolated, even if they wanted to be. Sheer survival
dictated that households share tasks in every realm of production. Later there were quilting bees, shared work toward an

object of beauty and utility. Maybe, we decided, talking about these books is a way of quilting, of weaving together the threads of our lives.

We're not formal in the dictionary sense. We do respect and adhere to the opening-question format. Beyond that, we have no procedural requirements. We all speak when we wish. We listen respectfully. We blurt out indignation when we can't help it. Personal analogies enter into the discussion only insofar as they illuminate or bring the book to life.

There are but two "rules" that come to mind. The first, that we will discuss potential new members or visitors with the group—a certain intimacy prevails, and the effect of adding a new person needs to be carefully thought through. And the second, that we won't read books simply because we feel we should. We learned this one the hard way. (I suppose we *should* read Stendhal; we really *should* read this particular Woolf; I guess it's time for Faulkner.)

We read both fiction and nonfiction. At one point, we thought of setting up a formal rotation: fiction, nonfiction, biography. But our process works well as it is. We simply hash over suggestions made by any one of us, and then agree by consensus to read a particular book. I have a friend in a much larger group (twenty or so members) that meets once a month. They rotate responsibility for choosing a book—the group has to read whichever book the chooser selects. Perhaps we are less democratic—or perhaps our easy intimacy obviates a need for such a formal structure. I don't know how many books we've each chosen. It seems fairly equal. It's never been an issue.

We meet approximately once a month, on Sunday afternoon. We choose dates when we choose books. When we are well organized, we choose several books in advance. One year, we assigned dates to eight books during a single meeting. That's unusual. Right now we are in a month-by-month phase. We have several books on the back burner, and at each meeting we choose what we will read next.

We don't intentionally read more women authors than men, but a quick survey tells me the ratio is exactly two to one. It also tells me that we primarily are reading fiction. For me, "shoulds" are more prevalent with respect to nonfiction. I approach almost any good fiction with happy anticipation, while even the best nonfiction can seem like an assignment. This is important information. I need to know this. I *should* read this. Fiction offers other truths.

How well do we really know Clarissa Dalloway? Would we speak to her in the street? Would we recognize Jewel Bundren if we saw him? Would Emma Bovary have acted as she did were she alive here, now, in this day and age? Is her story and those of Anna Karenina and Edna Pontellier truly tragic? Were their choices a function of their times, or of their tragic characters? Is *A Thousand Acres* an Iowa tragedy?

We dragged ourselves kicking and screaming to Robert Bly, and even then only because we wanted to read *Women Respond to the Men's Movement* (a book whose editor, Kay Leigh Hagan, attended our discussion). We felt we should at least be educated skeptics. All of us disliked the misogynist slant we gleaned from our various brief encounters with Bly. Reading the book confirmed our suspicions—we could be justly smug.

We have profited greatly from our discussions of gender, from the books noted above, as well as by the works of Carol Gilligan, Sarah Blaffer Hrdy, Nel Noddings, and Mary Catherine Bateson. Do we see ourselves in the women we read about? Where and how do our lives intersect with theirs?

This book group has become both familiar routine and an important part of my life. I have even turned down jobs that would necessitate leaving the group. While change is a given in life, I find comfort in anticipating continuity. I envision us ten years hence—older, some of us with grown children, wiser, more patient, more compassionate, and more mindful of what it is to be human.

THERE ARE BETTER THINGS IN LIFE TO STOMP OUT ON

Emily Tennyson
Grosse Pointe Woods, Michigan

I find it a bit ironic that I'm in a literary group—a social organization devoted to the Pursuit of Literary Excellence, or some such concept. I *really* love soap operas, "Entertainment Tonight," and *Star* magazine, and my friends always call me to find out the latest celebrity gossip. I'm not proud of my penchant for trash, but knowing me is like having a friend who always has a stash of Hershey Kisses—you know where the junk is when you want it.

In truth, we're just a bunch of females ranging in age from thirty-six (me) to mid-sixties. And, with the exception of one pompous individual, no one has great designs on a career as a literary critic. We just like to read. The group is about ten years old—an offshoot of a fairly old organization devoted to "women in the arts." (It sounds a bit grand, like finishing school and ladies' luncheons, but it's actually quite enjoyable.)

Admittedly, tastes vary. A few ladies are partial to fluffy books, like Anne River Siddons's *Outer Banks*, which I thought was an abysmal piece of crap. Fun suntanning book, but please don't tell me that's literature—it's designer sex. We take turns selecting books, which means we get a mix of best-sellers and classics. Generally, one person acts as critic and invites reactions from the others—we all feel comfortable voicing our opinions. I've been a critic for another book I thought was less than fabulous, and I had *no* qualms about sharing my opinion with the group.

The author of that book was a local Detroiter and faculty member at a community college, who published his novel via vanity press (excuse me, but *big deal*). He also happened to be a colleague of the pompous individual. My candor rankled her. Drawing herself up, she said, "I think it's just fabulous that he wrote this book at all. He should be commended for completing a work. I know it's taken me years to complete my second novel. That's because I'll soon be dean at the community college." When I told her that we were gathered together to do more than simply cheerlead folks who typed two hundred pages, she gave me a really dirty look. But I noticed that a few sideliners on the couch, who were eating the M&Ms furnished at every meeting, smiled in approval. On to the next book— *The Novel* by James Michener. To quote those men on film from "Living Color," *hated it.*

Sometimes we read a surprisingly controversial book with absolutely no sympathetic characters, like Mary Morris's *A Dangerous Woman*. During that discussion, people screamed instead of politely stating their opinion in three minutes or less, and the protocol-hungry members even threatened to walk out. (We're supposed to take turns and let everyone speak and not be rude.) The disagreement centered on the main character, Ruth, who had murdered someone. One faction said Ruth was a horrible person who deserved to go to jail, while another group had some sympathy for her and felt her position as one of society's underlings had driven her to the terrible deed. One group member rattled off some clinical psychological terminology—Ruth had "attention deficit disorder and was borderline schizophrenic." Maybe so, but I just thought she was one of nature's lost. The discussion got pretty ugly, and some people left. I think there are better things in life to stomp out on, so I ignored the tirade. A book group is meant to be fun, not a source of angst.

Then there are the surprising books that, unexpectedly, everyone enjoys. Fannie Flagg's *Daisy Fay and the Miracle Man*, a sweet look at adolescence in the deep south (I know that sounds like a Hallmark dustjacket, but it's true) was that kind of book for us.

Our group also holds a book exchange at Christmas. It's a free-for-all where you can steal anyone's book as long as she's not looking. It sounds complicated, and it is, but I got four really good books last year, and no one got hurt.

Next month we're reading, at my request, *Quartet in Autumn* by Barbara Pym. It's my *most* favorite book, and the meeting is at my house, and I'm the critic. I'm already warning myself not to become emotional when the pompous individual says that she can't believe we're reading a book about four English retirees who eat tinned meat. I'll just tell her she can take her deanship and shove it—that's fair, isn't it?

I'm really not very literate, although I spent ten years editing ponderous reference books on literary criticism. In many ways, it was a pleasant, albeit low-paying, existence. I read books about George Sand and Charles Dickens, which I liked, although I read so many of them that after a while they all ran together and became meaningless. My friends and I were fonts of information about Russian radical critics (Vissarion and "the boys," we called them), and I can still tell you which French poets took drugs and then had feverish deathbed conversions to Catholicism. I also spent a lot of time reading the Library of Congress directories to determine first publication dates, and got into disagreements with those who felt I wasn't as "committed to accuracy" as they. (They were probably right, by the way.)

After leaving the editorial world, I read only *National Enquirer* and *People* for an entire year. Then I joined my book group. I was worried it would be "déjà vu all over again" (I'd already spent too many years arguing about whether romanticism should be capitalized), but it's been an experience I really like.

FEMINIST BOOK DISCUSSION GROUP

Henrietta Bensussen with Sandra Miller
San Jose, California

The feminist book group began on a hike in the spring of 1985. I spent a good portion of this hike talking to Karen, whom I had just met. After we shared problems about parenthood and the good and bad points of living with a partner, we talked about books. She said she'd always wanted to be in a book group. I said, why not put a notice in our community newsletter and form one?

After the notice was printed, Karen received a number of phone calls from interested women. We had our first meeting with a discussion of Judy Grahn's *Another Mother Tongue*. Of the original seven or eight members, most are still active, though Karen has moved out of the area. At our first meeting, we decided on our group name and also decided that any book chosen for discussion would have to have a feminist viewpoint. While most of our members are lesbians, the group is open to any woman who identifies herself as a feminist.

We meet monthly in each others' homes on Thursday evenings between 7:00 and 10:00, rotating in a twenty-mile radius around San Jose. Currently, we have ten members, some of whom faithfully attend every meeting, others who show up sporadically. Refreshments are sometimes elaborate, other times tea and cookies.

Over the years, we've solved two major problems that could have destroyed the group. One was a personality clash, the other a love affair. Shortly after the group began, a new member joined. She held many strong opinions, as did Karen. One of the meetings ended in a shouting match between these two argumentative, volatile easterners. The rest of us mellower Californians sat back and tried to keep things from blowing up.

Afterward, we agreed that while Karen defended her opinions emotionally, she also respected the opinions of others. The new member, on the other hand, seemed to want to bludgeon people into agreement. At the next meeting, we set the rule that members must not attack each other, but keep to the topic and allow room for alternative points of view. The new member, not agreeing with the need for the new rule, dropped out.

A year or so later, Karen's partner, Sandy, who had been active in the group since its beginning, brought a new member, X, to the group. X became a regular, and Sandy broke up with Karen to start a household with her. That affair ended, acrimoniously, in record time. A few months later, Sandy went back to live with Karen in the house they still owned jointly. During this period, X, who was hosting a meeting of the group, refused to allow Sandy to attend.

Thus the issue of deciding who could host a meeting and who could participate or be denied an invitation to attend was forced upon us. We decided that meetings had to be held in neutral homes. Neither X nor Sandy and Karen could have meetings in their homes anymore. Very soon, X dropped out, saying she didn't have time to read. This was a relief to everybody.

Other women have joined the group with hopes of meeting a lover, but these predatory members usually drop out quickly. Our group meets to discuss books. Other agendas ultimately don't fit.

Our discussion is mostly conversational, but sometimes we'll start off with an in-depth, scholarly review we've read. For the first few years, our reading often led us to talk about our current lives, coming-out stories, family backgrounds, and problems at work. We've had some particularly deep discussions—these happen spontaneously and are dependent on members' reactions to a book. The most recent of these occurred after reading *Closer to Home: Bisexuality and Feminism*. Only five members were present at this meeting, all of whom had been in the group for some time. This created a feeling of intimacy and trust, and we opened up to each other around the issues of bisexuality and transsexuality within the lesbian community.

Sometimes we read a book that half the group loves and the other half can't relate to, and then the discussion revolves around that split. Sometimes we have potluck nights. On Erotica night, we all brought our favorite erotic books and read passages from them—we also brought something chocolate to share. On Spirituality night, similarly, we read from books that had informed our spiritual lives. These are two areas that seem to polarize people, so sharing our likes this way works better than trying to choose books that we can all agree to read.

We choose books by consensus. Someone will suggest a book and her enthusiasm will sell it to the others, or a review will spark interest, or the author will be someone we respect. There are always some members who don't get around to reading the whole book, or even more than the first chapter, but they do contribute to the general discussion in their reactions to points that are brought up. We like to alternate a "heavy" or nonfiction book with something lighter. We try not to read more than one, or at most two, books by the same author. Sonia Johnson is the only author for whom we've broken this rule. But after all, she is on the cutting edge of feminism.

To sum up our group—we are women who read books by feminist authors; we do not trash each other in discussions; we show respect for each others' opinions; we choose books by consensus; we are not rigid; and we try to find good solutions to problems that might otherwise break us up.

One of our members, an independent woman, is in a wheel-chair. We look out for her arrival and help pull her and her chair up steps. We make sure she gets settled in her car after the meeting. Helping, caring, thinking, and discussing—that's the Feminist Book Discussion Group.

MEETING BILL

Katheryn Krotzer Laborde
River Ridge, Louisiana

This story starts with three bored twentysomethings looking for some intellectual stimulation and a reason to
gather on a regular basis.

I doubt we would have met Bill any other way.

One muggy September night, Doug—somebody I'd known
since my freshman year of college—called out of the blue,
saying he wanted to form a book discussion group. At about
the same time another friend, Gina, claiming her brain was
turning to mush, came upon the same idea. I got the two
together, along with some others, and our group was born.

Altogether there were about ten of us—all with liberal arts
educations we failed to use in occupations that bored us. We
decided to meet every other Tuesday and drew up a prelimi-
nary book list. We agreed to read Kate Chopin's *The Awakening*—something short to get us started—for our first official
meeting, which we set two weeks from that night.

The big night came. Five people showed up.

"We need some outsiders, some new blood," Gina said, and we agreed. I designed a flier that we placed in a few coffee-houses around New Orleans. The flier was noticed: I received one death threat (complete with heavy breathing), and one query from a guy named Bill. I told him to read Anne Rice's *Interview with a Vampire* for Tuesday.

I told the three who showed up that night of our lone response. We ordered coffee and scones and agreed that, should this Bill turn out to be weird (remember that death threat), we would change our meeting spot and conveniently forget to inform him. We looked around anxiously. Doug announced that the newcomer was already fifteen minutes late and would perhaps never show. Then, as if on cue, the door edged open and a chubby man carrying a worn paperback looked anxiously about.

"Bill?" I called out to him and motioned to an empty chair. He sat, blinking as we introduced ourselves.

None of us was prepared for Bill. He was older by a good fifteen years, sporting more than a few gray hairs. He was pudgy and soft and had an intense squint. As the night wore on, he rubbed his palms along his thighs frequently and constantly pushed his glasses up. When he got nervous, he stuttered. Softly.

But he knew books—the great and the insignificant, the classic and the just-published. And while he was timid, he was insightful.

"If you d-don't mind," he said after the third meeting, "we need to revise this b-book list." He was right, of course, since the group had already lost more than half its original, enthusi-astic core. "W-why should I read something suggested by someone who's not even here?"

I opened my book and recorded the new list on the back cover. Some suggestions stayed the same. Deanne still wanted to read *Cold Sassy Tree*. Gina suggested *The World According to Garp*. Doug insisted we would love *Murder in the Smithsonian*. And I maintained that a discussion of *Edie*, accompanied by a viewing of the cult film *Ciao! Manhattan*, would give greater insight to a decade that most of us had seen through Mr. Rogers's eyes.

Then we got to Bill. "W-well, those are OK, but there are a few books I know of that I think you'd like." *The Unbearable Lightness of Being, Justine, The Last Temptation of Christ.* "The movie's coming out soon," Doug said. "Oh, but there's no way the movie could be as beautiful as the book," Bill countered. And, of course, he was right.

Deanne left the group before we could get to her book, so we never read it—nothing against Olive Ann Burns. And we found ourselves adding to and subtracting from the official list so often that I never bothered to retype it. All Gina had to say was, "Garcia Marquez's new book is in paperback," and we found ourselves adding *Love in the Time of Cholera* to the list. I can still remember the heated discussion over the success of that book's ending, with the men defending its romantic beauty, and Gina and I denouncing it as sentimental. What wouldn't be after reading *One Hundred Years of Solitude?*

That wasn't the only book to provoke us. On more than one occasion, I noticed people staring as we debated a particular point. *In Cold Blood* led to a discussion of capital punishment. We couldn't pick a mutual favorite from the *Best American Short Stories* anthology. Bill was the only one to enjoy *Forrest Gump,* and I recall being the lone defender of *A Cannibal in Manhattan.* And on one night, we were ten minutes into a discussion before realizing that Bill had read Steinbeck's *Cannery Row* rather than *Tortilla Flats,* the book *he* had suggested.

As the weeks passed, we got to know Bill better than we initially had thought possible. He told us stories about a younger, thinner Bill who wore his hair long and hitchhiked across the country. Occasionally he would talk about how he had waited out Vietnam in Canada, or how his trench coat and bike were, at one time, his only possessions. He mentioned that while his estranged wife was living in Alabama, he still worked for his father-in-law as a roofer. Though we all hated our jobs, we felt the worst for Bill since his was tearing him apart. We saw him as a teacher. A wonderful teacher.

And a frustrated writer. He told us about living in a boardinghouse that was occupied, for the most part, by old people. It wasn't until one of the tenants died, an old lame man whom

he used to visit, that Bill discovered the man was the estranged husband of the woman who ran the house. "I've always
wanted to write about that, but I've n-never known how," he said.

It turns out we all wanted to write, so in addition to our
bimonthly book meetings, we added a few writing sessions.
On these nights, each handed his or her notebook to another
who would write an opening sentence. We would take these
sentences and build upon them for an hour, and then read our
work aloud over second cups of coffee.

I once handed my notebook to Bill, who wrote: "When I
was a kid, I remember riding down the highways out West and
seeing little white crosses on the side of the road where there
had been an accident."

Fiction must have offered Bill an escape from a life I could
barely imagine. I knew our group offered some sort of salvation to him. He looked forward to our meetings, and was often
not only the first to arrive, but the last to leave.

One night Bill announced the roofing company had gone
bankrupt, and that he was out of a job and broke. His wife was
willing to take him back, he said, and he would be leaving at
the end of the week.

He was telling us good-bye.

Though it didn't have to be, that was the last meeting for all
of us. Doug was considering a move to Miami, and Gina a
career change. I had been accepted to graduate school, which
I knew would take me away from the group in time.

About three years have passed since the group disbanded. I
haven't kept in touch with Doug. Gina and I still get together
to discuss books and life in general, and though we've never
heard from Bill, his name pops into our conversation from
time to time.

I still half-expect to find him sitting on the porch of the
coffeehouse, book open. Sometimes I think I see him in a
crowd—quickly, peripherally—the way you see someone who
has passed away. I remember asking a limousine driver if his
name was Bill. He said no, and being drunk on champagne and
the excitement of my wedding day, I decided my eyes were
playing tricks on me.

If I ever do see him again, I'll tell him that I've made the jump: I'm a writer now. That I'm still working on that story about the little white crosses on the side of the road. And that I'd like to write that other story for him—the one about the boardinghouse. It's a hard story to write, but I know one day I'll find the words.

Of course, I'll name the main character Bill.

WOMEN READING TOGETHER

Suzanne Heggie Werner
West Hartford, Connecticut

I remember the exact moment we became a group. It was in May, halfway through our ninth meeting. We had read Oscar Hijuelos's steamy novel *The Mambo Kings Play Songs of Love*, and we were delicately discussing the wide range of colorful terms the author used for male anatomy. There was a pause as we leafed through our copies of the novel, searching for more references. It was then that Laura leaned back into the sofa, "I don't know about you guys, but this book made me horny." Another pause, this one uncomfortable. And then we began to laugh—together and loudly—some of us nodding our heads in agreement, others pleasantly jolted by Laura's honesty. It was then that we became a group of women reading books together, not just a collection of individuals who met monthly for a literary discussion.

I have to admit that I was worried until that moment. At our first meeting in September, we all sat stiff and straight on my family room sofa and chairs, our hands wrapped tightly around warm mugs of decaffeinated Earl Grey, our legs crossed discreetly at knees or ankles. Everyone was politely friendly. I suppose to an onlooker our feelings of distance during the first meeting would have been hard to understand. After all, we are all married, white, middle-class women in our late twenties and early thirties. Most of us are originally from the Northeast, and we all live in and around Hartford, Connecticut. Each of us has at least one graduate degree, most of us a law degree, all of us small children.

We had much in common from the beginning, but we were far from a ready-made social club. Women differ more from each other now than they did thirty years ago. Perhaps our development into a group would have been smoother back then. Thirty years ago we probably would all have the same life—no graduate degrees (unless in education), children in elementary school, wood-panelled station wagons, tennis elbow. We would travel in packs, like our mothers did, divided only by our socioeconomic classes and religious backgrounds.

Today there is no guarantee that a random group of women have enough in common to fuel a five-minute conversation. But we weren't a random group. I had selected most of the women who were seated in my home. My motive in forming the group was purely selfish—I wanted to read and discuss challenging books with a group of women I liked and admired. They were women that I had met during my three years practicing law in Hartford, but for the most part, these women didn't know each other. And that first night, I was sure I had made a mistake. I saw only potential disaster as the feisty personalities began to assert themselves and the more reserved withdrew into silence. The conversation moved in fits and starts.

We found solace in our agenda. We were professionals. We knew what to do with an agenda. We decided to meet on the third Thursday of every month from 8:00 to 10:00 P.M. with the location rotating from house to house. The hostess would be responsible for sending out a notice before the meeting, reminding the members of the book we would be discussing, and providing directions. Perhaps because all of us had spent so many hours in lecture halls, we rejected a formal structure, foregoing designated discussion leaders.

At our meeting to set up the group, some of us arrived with suggestions for the reading list for our first six months. These ranged from *Ulysses* to *Scarlett*. Others came with a willingness to read anything. We were deferential, unwilling to disagree with someone we didn't know. Some of us regretted our agreeability a few weeks later when we gathered to discuss our first book.

Do not pick a book about God for your first book group selection. We made the mistake of choosing *When Bad Things Happen to Good People* by Rabbi Harold Kushner. We chose it from among the suggested books because it was short—an easy read for our first meeting.

Unfortunately, we didn't consider that there are few things more uncomfortable than discussing your religious beliefs with a group of people you don't know. Even after our discussion of the book, I was the only one who knew how religiously diverse we were. Our group consisted of two Roman Catholics (one devout), one Baptist, one Protestant married to a Jewish man, a Jewish woman married to a Catholic man (both of whom were now Congregationalists), three fairly observant Jews, a Roman Catholic converted to Judaism, and an atheistic Jew. By the end of the meeting, I had heard more about some people's religious convictions than I knew about my own. Others, however, had opened their mouths only to toss in more popcorn. It was a relief when we moved on to a relatively benign subject: politics.

After such an awkward beginning, I was surprised any enthusiasm remained, but the members continued to read and come to meetings, and gradually, very gradually, we began to know and like each other. It wasn't like making friends in college when you could stay up late drinking foul coffee and talking for hours while slumped on a dorm bed. None of us had the time or inclination for true confessions. Rather, we grew to know each other intellectually first and, only then, personally. We each grew to appreciate the way the others thought, spoke, and argued.

Although we had no formal discussion leader, our analysis was fairly thorough, moving from writing style to thematic devices. Personal details began to emerge in our literary discussions—one member shared her Irish family's attitude toward drinking in the context of James Joyce's *Dubliners*, others shared conversations they'd had with spouses during our discussion of Deborah Tannen's *You Just Don't Understand*.

I don't think any of us were looking for a support group. We are no-nonsense women. We don't whine. But the social aspect of our group has become an essential part of our evenings together. The group serves an information-sharing function that used to be performed by coffee klatches and domineering mothers. We share stories about child care and toilet training. (We have seen each other through six pregnancies in the past year alone.) We have argued presidential politics and commiserated with Anita Hill and each other over sexual harassment.

So after about twenty hours together, we experienced what I like to think of as our defining moment—the moment we became a group. I looked around the room after Laura's admission and saw a group of women sprawled over the furniture and stretched out on the carpet, laughing with food in their mouths. We were finishing each others' sentences. We were leaning toward each other when we talked, tripping over words in our rush to share our thoughts. We had evolved into a group.

We are entering our second year together. We have lost one member to a move, but added three others. The new members, a doctor, a psychiatric nurse, and an English teacher, are integrating themselves into the group, learning our names and professions and slipping into our conversational rhythms. I think they were surprised to learn that we had only been together for a year.

ELEVEN YEARS AND 133 BOOKS LATER

Mary Nell Bryant
Washington, D.C.

Almost eleven years ago, a small group of friends from the Library of Congress formed a book discussion circle, affectionately called Book Group. One hundred thirty-three books later, the group is still going strong, with enough change to keep it interesting and alive, and enough sameness to give it a comfortable old-shoe feel. In our tenure, we have grown as an ever-changing family, seeing babies born, members wed, and now, even a mother-daughter pair of attendees.

Our group has survived because, in the spirit of the times, we run on the principles of democracy taken to their logical extreme—loosely bridled chaos. We have few, if any, solid rules and absolutely no requirements or duties other than bringing a love of books and ideas to our meetings. No, there is not even the requirement of reading the book—coming for the camaraderie and to hear the discussion is often all that one can manage in a given month. Our members work full-time outside the home or have families, or both. Any tight, rule-laden structure would lead to the group's immediate demise.

Since meetings are held one evening a month in a member's home, a member's only potential responsibility is to occasionally host the group, though even this is done on a completely random and voluntary basis.

Our group has grown and changed over the years, as friends and friends of friends have been brought in, adding a welcome depth and breadth of experience to the group. Our members are not only librarians, but also writers, booksellers, and moms. We have evolved into an all women's group, not by intent, at first, but by default. For the first few years, men who expressed a desire to come were welcome, but never appeared. When after a number of years, a man once again asked to participate, our startled group decided to vote (democracy wins again). After a lively debate, we concluded that we liked what we had become, a ladies' book club, and so we remain.

Our discussions, carried on over a wealth of food and drink, often begin with issues of the day and gradually work their way into the book of the month. There is no leader, no one designated to have done extra homework on author or book. Spontaneity is the rule of the day. Often a member who has taken a particular liking to a book will bring in additional background materials to round out the discussion.

Our most lively and memorable exchanges occur when there is wide disagreement about a book. The two books, Peter Dexter's *Paris Trout* and Maya Angelou's *I Know Why the Caged Bird Sings*, draw on similar themes of racism and yet led to very different discussions. There was a wide divergence of opinion over Dexter's book, hence a long, rollicking free-for-all. Angelou's book, on the other hand, was universally loved, leading to little more than sedate rounds of praise. Differences of opinion are not taken as personal affronts, and years later, we still find ourselves laughingly sparring over titles and authors from previous years.

By the time we have finished discussing the book of the month, we are warmed up to move on to the most interesting part of the evening—the selection of next month's book. This is often the liveliest and most informative part of the evening. Each person gets the floor not only to nominate books for the group's official selection, but also to mention other books and authors recently read, enjoyed, or heard about. Many members bring books with them, and a combined show-and-tell and book exchange takes place. When all nominees for the next book are in, sales pitches and negotiations that would make any lobbyist proud take place. Several rounds of voting are often necessary to get a winner. Picking the date for the next meeting is no less challenging. That done, and with someone volunteering as host, the cycle is ready to begin again.

Many groups select several books at a time, or even select all books for the coming year. Some settle on themes to follow over a period of several months. But with our group, attempts to pair even two books together for two successive months have been heatedly rejected. As I've mentioned, we are freedom and democracy unchained. Are librarians really anarchists?

Several years ago, after reading our one-hundredth book, we took a look back at what we had read, what we had liked and disliked, and what we had learned. Our authors were a cosmopolitan bunch, representing seventeen nationalities. American and British authors predominated, but we sampled wares from Japan, Canada, France, South Africa, Czechoslovakia, China, Russia, and several Latin American countries. Fiction greatly outnumbered nonfiction, yet some of our liveliest discussions centered on the latter. Of our nine favorite books, three were nonfiction. As to gender, we were surprised to find that we had read an almost even number of male and female authors, with forty-three men and fifty-seven women represented. So much for accusations of reverse sexism.

Twelve of us, many from the original group, voted for their five favorite and five least favorite of the one hundred books. Only one book appeared in both the most-liked and least-liked categories—Penelope Lively's *Moon Tiger*. That said, dubious honors go to Marge Piercy's *Small Changes* (a hands-down winner in the worst category with votes from six of the twelve voters), Anne Rice's *Interview with a Vampire*, Florence King's *Confessions of a Failed Southern Lady*, the aforementioned

Moon Tiger, Peter Dexter's *Paris Trout*, Marguerite Duras's *The Lover*, William Boyd's *An Ice Cream War*, and Fay Weldon's *Down Among the Women*. In defense of these works, each book (with the exception of *Small Changes*) had its fans as well.

And now for the favorites. The runaway winner was Harriet Doerr's *Stones for Ibarra*, followed by *Moon Tiger*, then Wallace Stegner's *Crossing to Safety*, Marcel Proust's *Swann's Way*, Willa Cather's *Song of the Lark*, Isak Dinesen's *Out of Africa*, Beryl Markham's *West with the Night*, Barbara Pym's *Excellent Women*, and Nien Cheng's *Life and Death in Shanghai*.

Since the voting, we have gone on to read another thirty-three books—too soon for another tally, but not too soon for a few observations. The male/female author ratio is closer with sixteen males and seventeen females. The universe is expanding. We have added authors from Israel, Egypt, Australia, India, Poland, and Nigeria. Fiction still far outweighs nonfiction, though memoirs are popular. We have gone back to several authors repeatedly, giving an unofficial vote of confidence to their works. Those authors we have read twice include: Margaret Atwood, Anita Brookner, Robertson Davies, Larry McMurtry, Toni Morrison, Jane Smiley, Wallace Stegner, Amy Tan, Anthony Trollope, Eudora Welty, and Virginia Woolf. The only two authors we have chosen three times are Anne Tyler and Willa Cather. Oddly enough, though we selected Anne Tyler three times, none of her works singly made it onto the best-loved books list.

Eleven years and 133 books later, what have we learned? We have learned, I think, not only of literature, but of diverse cultures and times. We have learned the broadening powers of discussion and found an acceptance and appreciation of different opinions. We have reaffirmed the value of fellowship and friendship. Yes, I think we will make it to two hundred books, and then we will look back once again to see where we've been.

SERIOUS COMMITMENTS

Curt Matthews
Evanston, Illinois

Four married couples meeting monthly for fourteen years to discuss books; a statistical improbability certainly, given the rate of divorce in America, but also perhaps a little dull? Not at all. The meetings are eagerly anticipated, the discussions lively, intense, often funny, sometimes heated.

The rules for the group are simple but stringent. Each member in turn chooses the book to be read. In the early years the books were chosen by consensus, but when it became clear that one member of the group did not think women were capable of writing important books, at least the ones he wanted to read, we switched to individual selections.

The assurance of a very good dinner is no small part of the appeal of our group. The meetings are held at the house of each couple in turn, with the hosting couple supplying the main course, the others bringing either the dessert, the appetizers, or the salad. (Yes, it is true that the women do most of the cooking. We did briefly try having the men cook, but the results were highly regrettable; not, I think, because of a lack of effort, but because of a lack of skill.)

But here is the crucial rule: at the end of each meeting, the date of the next meeting is agreed on by all of the members. We aim to meet about once a month on a Saturday evening, but each member brings his or her calendar, and we do not give up until we fix a date where all can attend. What this means of course is that every member attends every meeting. The exceptions have been due to the birth of children and the death of parents. Recently one couple confused the date and failed to show. Their remorse was extreme.

The Saturday evening schedule, the trouble taken over providing a very good dinner, the obligatory attendance—these features are both the cause and the consequence of the attitude shared by the members that their book group is a serious commitment.

It had not occurred to me that a successful book group made up of middle-aged married couples was in any way remarkable until the editor of this book pointed out that ours was one of the very few she could turn up based on this antiquated social unit. The problem it seems is that one half of a couple is male, and that good conversation on a serious subject in a mixed group is impossible, either because the males rudely dominate the women or the women are too timid to express their opinions.

This stereotype holds more truth than it should, but certainly one of the main reasons for our group's success is that no member of it, male or female, would tolerate such nonsense. It would be an exaggeration to suggest that these couples have stayed together because of their participation in the book group; but it is by no means an overstatement to say that intellectual equality goes a long way toward explaining the stability of the participants' marriages. The media teach us that love is something experienced in California by teenagers with perfect teeth wearing very small bathing suits. As one approaches fifty such notions do not seem sufficient to support a marriage. The book group is a strong affirmation of commitment.

The group is made up of an artist, an architect, two publishers, three professors, and a lawyer. When the group was first formed we were in our early thirties and each couple had a child or two. The idea of starting a book group came from two of the women; the husbands were initially skeptical. This skepticism was based on the fear that the meetings would either degenerate into group therapy sessions, or, even worse, into high-minded, pretentious, "literary" discussions.

Perhaps these fears were legitimate, or perhaps they were the usual male sexist notions expressed in code. The real danger was that the professors and the lawyer, accustomed by their professions to talking rather than listening, might do too little of the latter. That this has not been a problem can only be ascribed to the fact that these individuals, very secure in their areas of expertise, have seldom felt the need to dominate the conversation.

There has been some problem getting the artist and the architect to speak out as often as everyone would like them to. Their work requires a strong visual sense while the other members of the group are in professions that primarily rely on verbal skills. The rest of us are careful to solicit their opinions. We want to know how the various issues discussed look to them.

What do we hope to get out of these conversations about books? The unexamined life is truly not much worth living. Great fiction is the best possible mirror in which to see one's self. In a good discussion group, the characters and incidents of a novel are reflected in multiple ways, giving a depth and perspective that cannot be achieved in solitary reading.

It also seems to be the case that we all read more carefully and critically when we know that we will have an occasion to discuss a book. A good reading requires that interesting observations and small points be worked into a coherent overview of the book—a sort of position on it. Often these positions do not at all agree, and interesting conversations ensue.

The nonfiction we choose to read is demanding. Most of it falls under the category of books we should have read but have never had the time, and we would never have made the time, were it not for our involvement in the book group. What we learn from this reading is worthwhile in itself, but there is a great additional advantage; it often turns out that discussion of nonfiction, like that of fiction, leads to the great questions of meaning, truth, and beauty. It is almost embarrassing to mention such things in a society where bumper sticker phrases such as "shit happens" and "life's a bitch and then you marry one" seem to cover all the possibilities.

A fair number of the books we have chosen were read by all of us in high school or college. A lot of great literature is wasted on the young. If you read *Anna Karenina* or *Civilization and Its Discontents* in your teens, you are likely to discover, on rereading them in your forties, that your understanding has been much deepened by experience. It is a fine thing in your forties to be reminded that age can bring insight.

The greatest benefits and pleasures experienced by the members of our group may be a consequence of its long continuation. Some of the individuals are close friends outside of the meetings, some are not. But after fourteen years of serious intellectual contact, we are all very familiar with each others' views on the "great questions," and also quite skillful at challenging them. Some examples of issues to which we return again and again: Does truth exist independent of one's cultural circumstances? Does beauty necessarily have a moral aspect? How do the characteristic attitudes of science square with humanistic and religious principles?

Stated so abstractly, these issues may seem a little dull. But when they arise in the course of discussions of great literary works—and when they are argued by individuals who understand the consequences, in their personal lives, of the positions they take on them—such issues can hardly be exhausted in a lifetime and often lead to much greater intimacy than is experienced in most merely social friendships. Can two people (say a husband and wife) be said to really know one another if these questions have not carefully been discussed between them?

THE ARTS
CLUB

Dorothy Winslow Wright
Honolulu, Hawaii

Honolulu is an ocean and a continent away from the small southern town in the Shenandoah Valley where I had my first introduction to the Arts Club. I still think it's odd that I, a Bostonian, had my awakening to the deeper meaning of books in such a place. Perhaps it was because I had been raised in a city where I had access to music and art, as well as all manner of books through the public library system, that I didn't feel pressured to gobble up "culture." It was there for me whenever I wanted it.

This was not the case in Waynesboro, Virginia, in the 1950s. The nearest bookstore was thirty miles away, and the underfunded library seldom had new titles. My awareness of the Arts Club was triggered by a chance remark a friend made about a best-seller. When I asked her where she got it, she told me it was through the Arts Club. The group, which stressed both fine arts and literature, ordered books in bulk, circulated them, and discussed them later.

Being new to the area and unaware of southern protocol, I blurted out my interest, hinting that I would like to join the club. I rattled on about the cultural doings in Boston and how I missed them. By sheer naïveté, I must have said the right things because a few weeks later, I received a formal invitation—a handwritten note on heavy ivory vellum paper—to become a member of the Arts Club. As I look back, I don't know why I was ever voted in. The members were the town elite—social and community leaders, artisans, and educators—most were graduates of fine southern colleges. On my acceptance, my name was tacked onto list number five. I was told I would receive a copy of the selected book and that I should read it within two weeks and be prepared to discuss it at the next meeting.

This is how it worked. Each year a committee selected the titles—half best-sellers, the others poetry and the classics ("to help us grow"). Seven copies of each title were ordered through a New York discount house (a rarity in those days). When the books came in, a reading schedule was taped inside each cover. Woe to anyone who forgot to pass on the book in time! At the end of the year, the books became part of our personal libraries. To be fair about who received what book, we picked numbers from a hat for choosing order.

I did little that first year but contribute to the discussion, and that only shyly. During the artistic programs, I listened, becoming aware of the determination of talented people to use their gifts wherever they happened to live.

The following year I had to take a turn as leader, a responsibility that intimidated me. I was the only member who was not a college graduate. Chandler's, the well-respected secretarial school I had graduated from in Boston, didn't carry much clout in Virginia. I felt pressured to do a first-class presentation and prove myself intellectually worthy.

My book was Anne Morrow Lindbergh's *A Gift from the Sea*. At that time I had a baby and two small children, and I lived in a house that never seemed big enough to meet the needs of my growing family. When I recognized this stage of my life in the author's depiction of the oyster shell, the book came alive for me. The more I studied the book, the more I recognized myself at different stages—the delicate sunrise shell reminded me of the pristine sweetness of a fresh relationship when I was younger. I also felt hope for the future, and a hint of what it would be like to be older when my children would be grown and gone. My understanding expanded as I read the small volume and creative ways of presenting it flashed in my mind. I had shells. Lots of them. I would mount them on cardboard, next to quotations from the book, neatly typed and glued in place. These props nudged me toward confidence.

This confidence grew as I read the author's other works—her adventure books detailing her flights with her famous husband, her autobiography, and a disturbing book about the kidnapping of the Lindbergh baby. By the time I finished my background reading and conducted the program, the Arts Club had fulfilled its promise to me. I knew the Lindbergh family well, and I had developed a healthy respect for Anne Morrow Lindbergh's philosophy of life. Inspired by the author's example, and believing her words, I realized that I, too, would continue to grow as a person no matter what the circumstances.

The following year, when I led a discussion of Aldous Huxley's *Brave New World*, I was comfortable in my role as leader, although the book was a mind-blower. It took me a while to catch on to the satire of Our Ford. Fortunately my husband, an engineer, caught it right away and helped me understand the reproduction theme of the book: babies created à la Henry Ford. New knowledge and sensitivity surfaced.

I envisioned workers on production lines when I saw shiny new cars displayed in showroom windows, keenly aware of how fortunate I was. I didn't have to solder wires into place again and again, day after day, without allowing my mind to wander. My mind was free to rove as I folded laundry or sewed buttons, tasks I could do when I chose, not when a piece of machinery demanded that I do it. No production line directed my life. I was free to think, to learn, and to appreciate what was around me—all seeds for the writing I would pursue later in life.

The Arts Club broadened me at a time when I might have become smaller. Since the membership included artists, musicians, ceramists, and poets, I became aware of the intertwining of the arts—with books at the core. Yet more seeds for future writing.

When my husband was first transferred, we began a series of moves up and down the East Coast, moving from small towns to bustling cities and back again. Once settled in a new home, my first venture was to the local library to check out the literary services it offered—story hours for my children, poetry groups, writing groups. I had many short, but warmly remembered, associations with such groups.

Over time I lost touch with the women in the Arts Club, yet I still feel a connection with them. They opened doors when I needed doors opened and honed my appetite for books—an appetite I still have. I no longer belong to an organized book group, but I read voraciously, thanks to Honolulu's excellent public library system. When I discover a new author, I read more of his or her works. I look up biographies. In other words, I follow the format that was ingrained in me when I belonged to the Arts Club.

FROM *MOLLOY* TO *MADAME BOVARY*— FROM BILLIARDS TO BLOOD ORANGES

Debby Mayer
New York City

A few years ago, my reading group met for its tenth anniversary. We're not a famous group, or one that's set out to read a particular literature—the Bible, or the works of Shakespeare. If anything, we're a reading-group-as-offshoot-of-romance. We began when two of us had just started living together. We thought, as one more improvement in our life, why not start reading together? It was easy enough to talk to friends about movies—people often saw the same movie in the same month—but seldom was everyone reading the same book. So Dan asked his old friend Paul, and I asked my coworker Linda, and we met in our kitchen one night to try to make some sense of Beckett's *Molloy* (I had recently read *Watt* and was curious about the rest).

We had such a great time struggling with *Molloy* that we decided we should meet once a month, and that next we would read a selection of poems by Robert Lowell. Linda invited Holly, who soon invited David. A year or so later we all invited Adele. We've had several guests over the years, and one part-time member, but the core group has remained at seven. What surprised us, and amused us too, was the gratitude people expressed when asked to join or visit our group, as if an invitation had come for something very special.

We don't consider ourselves special or even exacting. Only one of us *always* finishes the book. Another of us almost never finishes the book but comes anyway and we're glad he does. Another member more often reads *about* the book, rather than reading the book itself—a biography of the writer, or some criticism of the work—and we appreciate that perspective. If we read a book in translation, we don't care which one: three of our most interesting meetings were spent comparing our translations of *Madame Bovary*, *The Inferno*, and the *Decameron*.

Coordinating the evening's snacks with the setting of the book or the nationality of the writer is also appreciated, but naturally some people are more attuned to that than others. For many years we did not discuss movies or television or jobs until after 10:00 p.m., but I notice we're slipping a little on that.

Several years ago I gave a workshop to two counties' worth of librarians on how to set up a reading group in a library. I realized as I answered their questions that they worried they would have to *teach the book*. No one in our group worries about teaching the book. We don't have a leader, and we don't assign anyone to look up critical references. The meeting rotates from home to home, and the person who will host the next month's meeting chooses the book for that meeting. Our group represents dozens of years of post secondary school education, and we see no reason to repeat the experience.

Though we're a small enough group to let everyone speak without shouting, we're also large enough to include elements that tend to disagree violently. Three of us are older than the other three and have managed to transcend our classical educations by this point in our lives—I mean, we'd like to think there's more to literature than Henry James. We can never predict the response of the oldest member of our group.

For our fifth anniversary, Dan typed up a list of the books we had read, culled haphazardly from his desk calendars. By our tenth anniversary, five of our six households had home computers, so our list is now on disk. We spent as much time that night discussing the list as we did the book, which was *Portrait of a Lady* by you know who. All of us made the meeting, even if we hadn't finished the book that month or years before, in college.

Looking at the new list, we decided that within the 106 selections, those that had made the deepest impression fell into one of four categories: books we might not have looked forward to and were completely surprised by; books we had looked forward to and were rewarded by; books we knew nothing about and were thrilled by; and books chosen by someone else that we were dragged through kicking and screaming.

We usually read poetry and fiction because they offer the most to talk about, but even there the exceptions prove the rule: we tend to agree that our most wildly contentious meeting was over John Berger's *Ways of Seeing*, and among the books we remember best is *The Great War and Modern Memory* by Paul Fussell. On the other hand, a book by a popular economist drove us all to silence, and not one of us was able to finish a book by a distinguished poetry critic. We were tempted to write the author. It was the first time in eight years that *none* of us had finished a book, which we felt said more about the book than the readers.

We can't help but consider our list something of an achievement, but that wasn't the point in drawing it up. For us it combines the best aspects of a photo album and a reunion, with mere titles able to recall the highs and lows of our reading group life. For me the books on the list that get stars—and there are several of them—are those that I not only enjoyed, but also read only because someone else in the group had chosen them.

Among those books, nothing quite matches that first year of discovery, when we went on from Lowell to Calvino, then through a couple of rough months with Thomas Hardy and Malcolm Lowry before soaring again with Eudora Welty, Philip Larkin, and Heinrich Böll's *Billiards at Half-Past Nine* (see category three above). Then *The Blood Oranges* by John Hawkes (another big fight), and the year wound down with Conrad, Ibsen, and Merrill before it came alive again with *To the Lighthouse* and *The Waves*. Virginia Woolf was one of the writers we decided to read just to see what all the fuss was about and we were rewarded for it. Others have been *Tobacco Road* (holds up) and *The Group* (doesn't).

At least once in the ten years each of us has been guilty of using the group to read a book that he or she felt we *should* read. These were some of our least successful meetings, and the books that brought us down included *The Origin of the Species*, *Adam Bede*, and *The Education of Henry Adams*. For a while we considered reading a huge popular novel every summer, but no one wanted to waste a choice on it, so the idea doesn't even surface anymore. We haven't done well by the couple of mysteries we've tried; only four people showed up to discuss *The Spy Who Came in from the Cold*, and they spent much of the evening drinking Scotch and playing poker.

I realized early on that if I didn't choose a woman writer when it was my turn to choose, we wouldn't read any women writers. It wasn't a role I wanted, but neither did I want to spend every meeting talking about Peter Handke or Thoreau when we could also discuss Edith Wharton or Flannery O'Connor. This went on, I'm sorry to say, for almost four years, until women writers began to appear in other's choices. *The Memoirs of Hadrian*, not my idea, is a classic category three.

Not all of my friends are avid readers, and one of them asked me once, what if you don't have time to read a book that month? It's the reading group, I said. It meets the first Wednesday of the month. You buy or borrow the next book the day after that month's meeting. You *want* to read it, that's why you're in the group.

But it hasn't always been easy to keep a reading group afloat for ten years. Ours has lasted through the death of two parents, through one divorce, three marriages, and the birth of four children, including a set of twins. Three people have given up smoking. Everyone has either moved or renovated their home (or both), except for Dan and me, whose apartment remains unchanged, a sort of reading group memorial park. People have missed the meetings for months at a time, and the reading group has always been there when they came back.

The previous reading group year has been difficult for me, not only because I was becoming accustomed to a new working life, but also because of the choices—*The Periodic Table* (my fault), *Foxybaby*, Robert Burns's poems, *The House of the Spirits*. Month after month, no matter which writer or what country the group turned to, I always wished I were reading something else. Until August, when Paul chose *Their Eyes Were Watching God* by Zora Neale Hurston, another writer we tried just to see what all the excitement was about. During that beastly hot month, I scratched through dialect I found difficult at first, to find a jewel of a book, something beautiful and fascinating and completely new to me. Only four of us were able to meet, but we didn't play cards or talk about movies. Instead, we went over and over the book, marveling at what we had finally discovered.

Then we moved on to everyone's favorite part of the meeting. That's when the next month's host (who usually knows who he or she is by instinct) takes out a small notebook or a scrap of paper on which is listed five or six books. The chooser reads the titles and authors, and we listen. We'll vote if necessary, and the chooser has final say, but right then, what we love is listening to the possibilities.

Imagine a real estate agent opening the door on an empty apartment, or a host greeting you as you arrive at a party, and over his shoulder you spot. . . . Except this is better. You have a home. You do or don't have a lover. But this is *reading group*. This list offers your next voyage—your potential happiness for a month. A fresh paperback or library copy or some volume already tucked into your shelves, waiting for you.

Coda

In October 1992, instead of celebrating its fourteenth anniversary, my reading group gave up its ghost. Like most slow demises, this one was complicated and sad. I could say it started with the tragic death of one member's child, but that would be melodramatic and not quite true. That member kept reading, kept coming to meetings, eventually had another baby. But in the meantime another member, hampered by chronic illness, stopped coming. Another took a job at night and could only meet weekends. Three people began to live and work outside of New York City, so their attendance became sporadic. In short, we often didn't have a quorum, and we couldn't seem to find enough new people to revive the group. Yes, people were interested . . . and then they had to be out of town on business that week.

In retrospect, I'd stress that there are two requirements for a successful reading group: first, everyone has to be there, wherever there is, and willing and able to make the group a part of his or her intellectual life; and second, the choice of books should rotate on a regular schedule for members. That way, someone will have thought ahead about the next book, so the group isn't left floundering over half-hearted choices and, if the group embraces different intellectual views and philosophies—and let's hope it does—members will get recurring chances to be represented. With our group so small, the choices fell into a pattern, and at least one of us felt disenfranchised.

But we kept trying, for months, to find books in paperback that we all wanted to read and to schedule and reschedule meetings because we'd had so much fun reading and talking about books for more than ten years. We hated to let it end. At least three of us haven't—we're in new groups, still compiling that reading group life list.

DIGESTING THE BOOK

Lisa Goff
Charlottesville, Virginia

Before I moved to Charlottesville, I lived in Chicago. I joined a Book Club there—it was never given a fancier name—in March of 1988, four months after it was founded in November 1987. I was looking for a forum to discuss literature, something to replace the college classroom. I got much more than that. I got a group of new, accepting, and challenging women friends, an enhanced sense of belonging in the depersonalized business world, and a feeling of community with women whose experiences were myriad and yet in many ways very similar. And I read a lot of books I'd never have picked up otherwise.

While all of us joined for the books, in fact intellectual stimulation was only the jumping-off point for Book Club, the attraction that brought all of us together once a month for drinks, dinner, and conversation at a downtown hotel. The exchange of ideas, experiences, and stories was the ultimate attraction, and the glue that kept a group of sixteen or so very busy women committed to Book Club.

We were all fiercely engaged in writing our own lives, and our meetings once a month—through the vehicle of a book—helped us gain perspective. Along the way to talking about literature, we talked about life, which I think would make the authors of the books we read very happy indeed.

Let me emphasize, however, that Book Club was very much about books: we didn't degenerate into unfocused gab sessions about our lives and loves after a cursory examination of the text at hand. Quite the contrary. We hewed to the task of examining the book, discussing its merits as literature as well as its social or cultural aspects. Bits and pieces from our own lives were shared only in service to this goal. And it was that, I think, that unified the members and kept our Book Club going strong.

A few basic facts about our Book Club. It was formed in November 1987 by a woman who was head of the Chicago landmarks preservation council and who had recently moved to Chicago. She had been in a very active book group in San Antonio, and wanted to continue the tradition in her new home. Those first few members each asked a friend or two or, as in my case, were asked by friends if they could please join. Each potential new member was brought up very casually at the next meeting, invariably agreed upon, and asked to join. Soon the group had grown to almost twenty people.

Requests to join kept pouring in—I recruited a new member in exactly the same way I had been recruited, by singing Book Club's praises over lunch to a professional acquaintance-cum-friend, who then asked to join—but the group decided any more than sixteen or so was unwieldy. So we made a list of people who wanted to join and put them in touch with each other, and another book group was born. As our own members moved away—or didn't show up for more than six months—we replaced them with people remaining on the list.

All our members were women. More on this later. We met on the third Wednesday of every month in a spacious conference room of a downtown hotel, where we had an elegant dinner. This was generally agreed to be preferable to meeting in people's homes: no preparation, no clean-up. We split the nominal cost of the room rental and paid for our dinners, which came to about twenty-three dollars per meeting. Everybody paid their own wine tab.

We had a bank account in the name of Book Club and a treasurer who collected our checks at each meeting, dashing to the bank as it opened the next morning to deposit them before the check she wrote the hotel the night before had a chance to bounce. The only other "officer" we had was a secretary of sorts who sent out monthly notices of meetings and books scheduled.

At the monthly meetings, we had drinks from about 6:30 to 7:00 p.m., then discussed any outstanding business and proceeded to the discussion of the book by 7:15 or so. The salad was usually served at around the same time, and when dessert was finished around 9:00 p.m., we had digested the book as well.

Each month the book discussion was led by a member who had volunteered to research the book, the author, and anything else she deemed pertinent. At a minimum, the leader came armed with facts about the author and an outline of what she found most interesting about the book—talking points, in Washington parlance.

Some people went the extra mile. When we discussed the biography of Freud, the discussion leader brought along a psychologist to discuss the inapplicability of Freud in African cultures. The person who led the discussion of *West with the Night* brought her pictures of Kenya. The person who led John McPhee's *Pine Barrens* had done some reporting, calling up the Pine Barrens park ranger to get an update on the state of affairs in that natural area.

There was, of course, constant interruption from members with comments and ideas, which was generally encouraged. The discussion leader judged how far to let this roam, and when to drag everybody back to her agenda. But in general the discussions were free-flowing. They seemed to find their own groove, meandering around a point occasionally, but always finding their way back to the issue. The members were generous listeners, giving everyone a chance to make her point, but they also were at times provocative arguers. This never got to the point of bad temper, or even rudeness, but people with strong opinions didn't hesitate to air them. Always, however, there was an attitude of respect toward the people who disagreed.

For the most part, people came even if they hadn't read, or finished, the book. But ninety percent of the people at every meeting had read the book, so this never presented a problem.

We decided which books to read by a very disorganized process of suggestion and discussion that we staged once every few meetings, deciding on books for about three months in advance. We only read books that were in paperback, a cost consideration. The secretary kept a running list of suggestions, which she then tossed out the next time we discussed new books, by which time we had usually lost interest in the old suggestions and had a batch of new ones from which to choose.

Any book was fair game for consideration, as long as it was in paperback. We read mammoth eight hundred pagers and slim volumes barely long enough for the train ride home from work. We read feminist invective, mystery novels, philosophy, and classic nineteenth-century novels. The only book I remember getting hooted down for lack of substance was Donald Trump's *Art of the Deal*.

We read mostly fiction, with a fair helping of nonfiction. A listing of books read February to June 1989 is typical in its diversity: *The Chalice and the Blade*, *Interview with a Vampire*, *That Night*, *The Man Who Mistook His Wife for a Hat*, and *Love Medicine*.

Without a conscious effort, we read a lot of books by women authors. At one point, there was a conscious effort to include male authors, but if we weren't watching ourselves, we turned to female authors almost exclusively. This may have been an outgrowth of the all-women membership, which I'd like to say a few words about.

This was a very deliberate decision, to be all female. I never talked to the original founders about exactly why this occurred, but I can comment on the effects of all-woman membership, which I wouldn't have any other way.

As professional women, we were all painfully aware that even forceful, aggressive, highly paid professional women talked less in the presence of men. Men dominate discussions, period. We may not have liked it, but we recognized it. And a Book Club discussion was the last discussion we wanted to give men the chance to dominate.

Moreover, I think the women in Book Club enjoyed the freedom of expression afforded by the all-female forum (I know, I know: the guys who belong to those hideous all-male clubs say the same thing). Because we were all women, the agenda at each meeting was female-oriented. We were free to discuss the books from a female perspective without taking time out to defend our positions against a storm of male protest. And that was a nice break.

Many Book Club members became friends, often close friends, outside of Book Club, and over the years we became increasingly involved in each others' lives, celebrating weddings and babies, sharing problems and crises. But the monthly meetings remained our time to discuss books, how they made us feel, what emotions or associations they dredged up, how close the author came to accomplishing her or his goal, what heights the artistry did or didn't reach.

ONE GOOD BOOK
DESERVES ANOTHER

Lenore Baeli Wang
Somerville, New Jersey

After reading a line of poetry in *The Windhorse Review*—"A mushroom asks you to crouch low"—I picked up the pencil that's always at hand, whatever I'm reading, and filled the wide margin beside the poem with my own poetry—"A river asks you to peer in / a cloud asks you to lie down, look up. . . ."

When I closed *The Waves*, Virginia Woolf's poetic novel wherein the passage of time is described by the changing quality of light and cyclic tides, I found pen and paper and wrote a short story in which the passage of time revealed itself in my description of a drug addict's spoon, forgotten on a windowsill by all but the narrator. Its heroin-residual colors changed as the light changed, so I called the story "The Rainbow Spoon."

Rarely do I read anything without wondering what my own version would be. And it seems to be out of this practice that productivity comes for me. There even seems to be a proportional relationship.

Last year I attended a production of Shakespeare's *As You Like It*. The bad direction made me hungry for the original, so I reread the play. The rereading spawned ideas I hadn't gleaned from my first reading. I wondered what happened *after* the ecstatically happy ending. In the play, Phebe had been attracted to Rosalind when the latter was disguised as a man; Orlando was capable of slight attraction to Rosalind who pretended to be a man pretending to be a woman so that Orlando could practice wooing. What a lovely Shakespearian mess of sexual identity confusion. I felt it crying out to be continued, so I wrote a sequel, *Phebe and Rosalind*, that speculates what happens if we romantically love a person regardless of gender.

While I experience long blocks of writer's block now and then, I never experience reader's block. Reading, in fact, is the best cure for writer's block that I've ever known. I read with a pencil nearby or in hand. I read with an inventor's cap on my head.

If I'm intrigued by a book written by a living author, I write her or him through the publisher, and if I receive a letter back, more things happen. The book comes even more to life. After reading yet another collection of short stories by Alice Adams, I wrote to tell her that one of her stories inspired one of mine. She responded that her "stories are set off by what [she] reads." My suspicion confirmed by an author I respect, I pursued my habitual process of reading-to-write with renewed confidence.

Adrienne Rich has a line of poetry about "books that change us." Woolf writes about reading that leads to action, even if it's the reading of words posted in a railway car, "'Do not lean out of the window.' At first reading the . . . surface meaning is conveyed; but soon . . . we begin saying, 'windows, yes windows—casements opening on the foam of perilous seas' and before we know what we are doing, we have leant out of the window . . . looking for Ruth . . . amid the alien corn."

As a writer, the change and actions reading produces within me inevitably lead to or take the form of writing. The words Woolf reads on a train window transform into poetry once they're taken in and contemplated by her, much in the same way digestion improves the nutritional value of food we eat. And in the same way that if we don't eat, we don't live very long, if we don't read, how can we possibly write? Reading is the bread of my writing life, the cure for my writer's block. It is my only hope as a writer.

I have been in the midst of a block recently; I haven't had much time to read amidst a hectic semester of teaching. The one thing I did read during my long drive to work, however, in the side mirror of my car, waits patiently in the back of my mind for future use in some unknown piece of writing. "Objects in mirror are closer than they appear," it says. Surely there's a story or poem awaiting birth in that, I've been thinking. Or maybe I'm just starved for some good reading.

I did manage to read a line of Emerson, too (a line here, a line there; I take what I can get). "One must be an inventor to read well," he writes. After reading that, I'm moved to write that its inverse is equally true, "One must read well to be an inventor."

Toward a definition of reading that leads to writing, I offer Goethe's classification of three types of readers, "Some enjoy without judgment; others judge without enjoyment; and some . . . enjoy while they judge. The latter . . . reproduces the work of art on which it is engaged."

The first book I remember reading with intense passion is *The Brothers Karamazov*. On the last page of that now sixteen-year-old paperback I wrote—followed by an exclamation point—"The best book in the whole world!" Sometimes, after reading, that is the only writerly response.

PART II
Book Lists

Many of the lists that make up this section of *The Book Group Book* come from people whose essays are printed in Part I, though that's not always the case.

The lists are arranged in alphabetical order by contributor, and they come in all lengths and formats—for the most part, they're reproduced here the way they were submitted. Some are organized chronologically according to when a group read a particular title, others alphabetically by author. Some are grouped according to themes, others appear in random order. Some are annotated, with personal comments from the book group member as to how she or he liked the book and how it was received by the group, others are offered staccato style so that you can only guess at a group's reaction. Some have mini-introductions that explain a group's purpose and how it is organized, others leave us guessing on that end too.

You'll find some repeat titles among the lists, but the repetition can be instructive. As one book group member said to me, "When I told my friend who'd been in a book group for years that I had joined a group a few months ago, she was enthusiastic and encouraging and a little cynical. 'Let me guess,' she said. 'So far you've read *The Joy Luck Club* and *Remains of the Day*.' Well, she was right, but so what? I mean, sometimes everybody is reading the same books because the books are just too good to miss."

That said, any group looking to embellish its book list will find this section full of potential titles—enough thought-provoking reading to keep a group engaged and committed for years to come.

OBERLIN
BOOK CLUB LIST
Jeanne Bay and Shirley Johnson
Oberlin, Ohio

"**S**hirley's book club" (so named by the Oberlin Coopera-
tive Bookstore because Shirley did all the arranging with
them for selecting and ordering books) is just entering its
fourth decade. The founding group began by discussing Betty
Friedan's *The Feminine Mystique* and then branched out into
many other areas. Subjects? These vary considerably, as you
can see from our lengthy reading list. Sometimes we have a
theme—minorities, women authors, mother-daughter relationships; sometimes we focus on tried-and-true authors—
Cather, James, Faulkner. In general, our reading is eclectic and
includes fiction, essays, and biography. A combination of good
will, combativeness, humor, liveliness, and an element of un-
predictability have made this, over the years, a special group.

Woman in the Dunes, Kobo Abe
Second Chances, Alice Adams
Twenty Years at Hull House, Jane Addams

A Death in the Family, James Agee
Who's Afraid of Virginia Woolf?, Edward Albee
Of Love and Shadows, Isabel Allende
I Never Sang for My Father, Robert Anderson
Winesburg, Ohio, Sherwood Anderson
The Lark, Jean Anouilh
Surfacing, Margaret Atwood
Powers of Attorney, Louis Auchincloss
Dog Beneath the Skin, W. H. Auden and
    Christopher Isherwood
Emma and *Pride and Prejudice*, Jane Austen
Growing Up and *Good Times*, Russell Baker
Pere Goriet, Honoré Balzac
Kepler, a Novel, John Banville
Nightwood, Djuna Barnes
End of the Road, John Barth
Love Always, Ann Beattie
Virginia Woolf, Quentin Bell
The Victim, Saul Bellow
Love Is Not Enough, Bruno Bettelheim
Lying, Sissela Bok
Lost Honor of Katherine Blum, Heinrich Böll
A Man for All Seasons, Robert Bolt
Ficciones, Jorge Luis Borges
Miracle at Philadelphia and *Yankee from Olympus*,
    Catherine Bowen
The Death of the Heart, *Friends and Relations*, and
    The Little Girls, Elizabeth Bowen
The Desegregated Heart, Sarah P. Boyle
Three Short Novels, Kay Boyle
Joan of the Stockyards and *Mother Courage*, Bertolt Brecht
Tenant of Wildfell Hall, Anne Brontë
Jane Eyre and *Shirley*, Charlotte Brontë
Wuthering Heights, Emily Brontë
Still Life, A. S. Byatt

Women in Fiction, Susan Cahill, ed.

Exiles, The Plague, The Stranger, Caligula, and
  The Just Assassins, Albert Camus

The Homemaker, Dorothy Canfield

House of Children, Joyce Cary

Death Comes for the Archbishop, My Antonia, O Pioneers!,
  The Professor's House, and *Sapphira and the Slave Girl,*
  Willa Cather

Uncle Vanya and *Three Sisters,* Anton Chekhov

The Awakening, Kate Chopin

Taipan, James Clavell

Cheri, Colette

Family Happiness, Laurie Colwin

Mrs. Bridge, Evan S. Connell

Lord Jim, The Secret Agent, Heart of Darkness, Youth, and
  Typhoon, Joseph Conrad

Stop-Time, Frank Conroy

Road from Coorain, Jill Ker Conway

Great Short Works, Stephen Crane

A Woman's Place, Anne Crompton

Madame Curie, Eve Curie

Memoirs of a Dutiful Daughter, Simone de Beauvoir

Year of the Zinc Penny, Rick DeMarinis

Moll Flanders, Daniel Defoe

White Noise, Don DeLillo

Bleak House, Charles Dickens

White Album, Joan Didion

Pilgrim at Tinker Creek and *An American Childhood,*
  Annie Dillard

Seven Gothic Tales and *Out of Africa,* Isak Dinesen

Lincoln Reconsidered, David H. Donald

Crime and Punishment and *The Idiot,* Fyodor Dostoevsky

Sister Carrie, Theodore Dreiser

The Visit, Traps, The Pledge, and *The Physicists,*
  Friedrich Dürrenmatt

A Matter of Principle, Donald Dworkin
Disturbing the Universe, Freeman Dyson
The Solace of Open Spaces, Greta Ehrlich
Middlemarch and *The Mill on the Floss*, George Eliot
The Invisible Man, Ralph Ellison
Silence, Shusaku Endo
The Trojan Women, Euripides
Five Smooth Stones, Ann Fairbairn
Absalom, Absalom!, *Light in August*, *Sartoris*,
   The Sound and the Fury, *The Unvanquished*, and
   Go Down Moses, William Faulkner
Joseph Andrews, Henry Fielding
The Great Gatsby, F. Scott Fitzgerald
Madame Bovary, Gustave Flaubert
Mary Wollstonecraft, Eleanor Flexner
The Good Soldier, Ford Madox Ford
Howards End, *The Longest Journey*, *A Passage to India*,
   and *A Room with a View*, E. M. Forster
The French Lieutenant's Woman, John Fowles
Thaïs, Anatole France
Man's Search for Meaning, Victor Frankel
My Mother, Myself, Nancy Friday
The Feminine Mystique, Betty Friedan
The Art of Loving, Erich Fromm
Overhead in a Balloon, Mavis Gallant
One Hundred Years of Solitude, *No One Writes to the
   Colonel and Other Stories*, *The Autumn of the Patriarch*,
   and *Love in the Time of Cholera*,
   Gabriel García Marquez
Nickel Mountain, John Gardner
North and South, Elizabeth Gaskell
The Balcony, Jean Genet
Lafcadio's Adventures, Andre Gidé
The Trouble in One House, Brendan Gill
The Odd Women, George Gissing

Electra, Jean Giraudoux

Schools without Failure, William Glasser

The Inheritors, Lord of the Flies, and *The Spire*,
    William Golding

The Vicar of Wakefield, Oliver Goldsmith

World of Strangers and *A Sport of Nature*,
    Nadine Gordimer

Final Payments and *Men and Angels*, Mary Gordon

The Keepers of the House, Shirley Grau

World Without End, Francine du Plessix Gray

In This Sign, Joanne Greenberg

I Never Promised You a Rose Garden, Hannah Green

The Best and the Brightest, David Halberstam

In Search of Salinger, Ian Hamilton

*Jude the Obscure, The Mayor of Casterbridge,
    Tess of the d'Urbervilles*, and *Under the Greenwood Tree*,
    Thomas Hardy

Seduction and Betrayal, Elizabeth Hardwick

The Other America, Michael Harrington

Decision, Richard Harris

The Go Between, L. P. Hartley

The Marble Faun and *The House of Seven Gables*,
    Nathaniel Hawthorne

The Transit of Venus, Shirley Hazzard

Writing a Woman's Life, Carolyn Heilbrun

Catch 22, Joseph Heller

Pentimento, Lillian Hellman

No Man's Land: The Last of White Africa,
    John H. Heminway

Siddhartha and *Steppenwolf*, Herman Hesse

The Deputy, Rolf Hochhuth

Private Memoirs: Confessions of a Justified Sinner,
    James Hogg

Hazards of New Fortune and *The Rise of Silas Lapham*,
    William Dean Howells

Doll's House, *Hedda Gabbler*, and *Rosmersholm*,
  Henrik Ibsen
The Remains of the Day, Kazuo Ishiguro
Soledad Brother, George Jackson
The Ambassadors, *The Aspern Papers*, *Portrait of a Lady*,
  Washington Square, *The Turn of the Screw*,
  Wings of the Dove, *The American*, *The Golden Bowl*,
  and *Spoils of Poynton*, Henry James
Pictures from an Institution, Randall Jarrell
Country of the Pointed Firs, Sarah Orne Jewett
Heat and Dust and *Out of India*, Ruth Prawer Jhabvala
Foxybaby, Elizabeth Jolley
Fear of Flying, Erica Jong
A Portrait of the Artist as a Young Man and *Dubliners*,
  James Joyce
The Trial, Franz Kafka
Sound of the Mountain, Yasunari Kawabata
Freedom or Death, Nikos Kazantzakis
Annie John and *Lucy*, Jamaica Kincaid
The Woman Warrior and *China Men*,
  Maxine Hong Kingston
A Not Entirely Benign Procedure, Perri Klass
Age of Longing and *Darkness at Noon*, Arthur Koestler
On Death and Dying, Elizabeth Kubler-Ross
Laughing Boy, Oliver LaFarge
The Leopard, Giuseppe di Lampedusa
The Quest, Elizabeth Langgasser
Sons and Lovers, *The Plumed Serpent*, and *Women in Love*,
  D. H. Lawrence
Martha Quest and *The Golden Notebook*, Doris Lessing
Balm in Gilead, Sara L. Lightfoot
The Natural, Bernard Malamud
The Autobiography of Malcolm X, Malcolm X
Man's Fate, André Malraux
The Watch that Ends the Night, Hugh MacLennon

Death in Venice, Thomas Mann
Nectar in a Sieve, Kamala Markandaya
Bird of Life, Bird of Death, Jonathan Maslow
The Folded Leaf and *They Came Like Swallows*,
  William Maxwell
Memories of a Catholic Girlhood, Mary McCarthy
Principles of American Nuclear Chemistry,
  Thomas McMahon
Testing the Current, William McPherson
Blackberry Winter, Margaret Mead
The Confidence Man, Herman Melville
Growing Up Female in America, Eve Merriam, ed.
Death of a Salesman, Arthur Miller
Spring Snow, Yukio Mishima
Dangerous Dossiers, Herbert Mitgang
Love Among the Cannibals, Wright Morris
Song of Solomon and *The Bluest Eye*, Toni Morrison
The Flight from the Enchanter and *The Severed Head*,
  Iris Murdoch
Speak, Memory, Vladimir Nabokov
India—A Wounded Civilization and *A Bend in the River*,
  V. S. Naipaul
The Vendor of Sweets, R. K. Narayan
Portrait of a Marriage, Nigel Nicholson
The Octopus and *McTeague*, Frank Norris
Expensive People, Joyce Carol Oates
Three Plays, Sean O'Casey
White Lantern, J. Leonard O'Connell
Tell Me a Riddle, Tillie Olsen
Mourning Becomes Electra, Eugene O'Neill
Keep the Aspidistra Flying, George Orwell
My Michael, Amos Oz
I Remember, Boris Pasternak
A Short History of a Small Planet, T. R. Pearson
Manchester Fourteen Miles, Margaret Penn

Naked Masks, Luigi Pirandello
The Bell Jar, Sylvia Plath
Presidential Elections, Nelson W. Polsby and
   Aaron Wildavsky
The Old Order, Katherine Ann Porter
My Name Is Asher Lev, Chaim Potok
Swann's Way, Marcel Proust
Quartet in Autumn, Barbara Pym
The Negro in the Making of America, Benjamin Quarles
Beyond Vietnam, Edwin Reischauer
Smile Please, Jean Rhys
Rabble in Arms, Kenneth Roberts
Survive the Savage Sea, Dougal Robertson
Housekeeping, Marilynne Robinson
Jean Christophe, Romain Rolland
Boss, Mike Royko
Autobiography (Volume 1), Bertrand Russell
Home, Witold Rybczynski
The Man Who Mistook His Wife for a Hat and
   A Leg to Stand On, Oliver Sacks
Mrs. Stevens Hears the Mermaid Singing and
   History of a Man, May Sarton
Memoirs of a Fox-Hunting Man, Siegfried Sassoon
A Fine Romance, C. P. Seton
Major Barbara, Heartbreak House, and *St. Joan*,
   George Bernard Shaw
And Quiet Flows the Don, Mikhail Sholokhov
Orphans, Real and Imaginary, Eileen Simpson
Spinosa of Market Street, Isaac Bashevis Singer
Walden Two, B. F. Skinner
The Russians and *Power Game*, Hedrick Smith
Humphry Clinker, Tobias Smollett
Cancer Ward and *The First Circle*,
   Alexander Solzhenitsyn
Electra, Sophocles

Memento Mori and *A Far Cry from Kensington*,
  Muriel Spark
Salt Line, Elizabeth Spencer
The Education of a Wasp, Lois M. Stalvey
Angle of Repose and *The Spectator Bird*, Wallace Stegner
Three Lives, Gertrude Stein
Rosencrantz and Gildenstern Are Dead, Tom Stoppard
Never Done, Susan Strasser
Pioneer Women, J. S. Stratton
Alice James, Jean Strouse
Lie Down in Darkness, William Styron
The Kingdom and the Power, Gay Talese
The Joy Luck Club, Amy Tan
Angel, Elizabeth Taylor
Old Forest and Other Stories and *A Summons to Memphis*,
  Peter Taylor
The White Hotel, D. M. Thomas
Lark Rise to Candleford, Flora Thompson
The Eco-Spasm Report, Alvin Toffler
Anna Karenina and *War and Peace*, Leo Tolstoy
Middle of the Journey, Lionel Trilling
Barchester Tower, Anthony Trollope
A Connecticut Yankee in King Arthur's Court, Mark Twain
The Accidental Tourist and *Breathing Lessons*, Anne Tyler
Kristin Lavransdatter, Sigrid Undset
On the Farm, John Updike
A Far-Off Place, Laurens Van der Post
Galapagos and *Slaughterhouse Five*, Kurt Vonnegut
The Color Purple and *The Third Life of Grange Copeland*,
  Alice Walker
All the King's Men, Robert Penn Warren
A Handful of Dust and *Decline and Fall*, Evelyn Waugh
Marat/Sade, Peter Weiss
The Hearts and Lives of Men, Fay Weldon

The Optimist's Daughter, Thirteen Stories, and
  Golden Apples, Eudora Welty
The Devil's Advocate, Morris West
The New Meaning of Treason and *The Real Night,*
  Rebecca West
Roman Fever, The Age of Innocence, and
  The House of Mirth, Edith Wharton
Points of My Compass, E. B. White
Solid Mandela, Patrick White
One Generation After, Elie Wiesel
Incline Our Hearts, A. N. Wilson
The Quest for Christa T., Christa Wolf
Look Homeward Angel, Thomas Wolfe
Mrs. Dalloway, To the Lighthouse, The Waves, and
  Three Guineas, Virginia Woolf
A Coin in Nine Hands, Marguerite Yourcenar
The Masterpiece, Émile Zola

BOOK
LIST

Ellie Becker
Santa Fe, New Mexico

1988

The Unbearable Lightness of Being, Milan Kundera. Men, women, love, freedom, necessity, political repression, moral truth. Elicited either strong like or dislike.

Beloved, Toni Morrison. Haunting, deep discussion of humanity, mother, dignity, truth, the black woman's experience. Profound.

In a Different Voice, Carol Gilligan. Questions about dividing up and determining moral choices on the basis of gender.

Love in the Time of Cholera, Gabriel García Marquez. Lost in the magic of Garcia Marquez, surreal. Where will Fermina and Florentino end up? Or will they end?

1989

The Drama of the Gifted Child, Alice Miller. Implications for our own children, for all children. How do we raise whole human beings?

The Woman That Never Evolved. Sarah Blaffer Hrdy. Why are female reproductive organs hidden? Does the female primate choose the father of her offspring? Which tends more toward monogamy, male or female? Who's in charge here, anyway?

A Room of One's Own, Virginia Woolf. Difficult, but worth it.

Jacob's Room, Virginia Woolf. Almost incomprehensible.

Breathing Lessons, Anne Tyler. Disappointing. Superficial. As one member noted, doesn't say much for the Pulitzer.

1990

Ceremony, Leslie Marmon Silko. Extraordinary. Moving. Violent.

Caring: A Feminine Approach to Ethics and Moral Education, Nel Noddings. Better scholarship than the Gilligan. Cogent. Moral choices. Are imperatives ethical?

The Road from Coorain, Jill Ker Conway. A pleasing biography. The effects of constraint, bias, education, and harsh landscape on a woman of courage.

The Bone People, Keri Hulme. Strange, almost eerie. Unusual style—the literal part is difficult, but a deeper level is experienced.

Woman at Otowi Crossing, Frank Waters. Uninspired by the writing, intrigued by the time, place, history, and woman. Desire to read other versions by other authors.

Sons and Lovers, D. H. Lawrence. Vintage Lawrence: mother, woman, love, violence. Is anyone likeable in this book?

The Mill on the Floss, George Eliot. Dissatisfying. Much inferior to *Middlemarch.* Copout ending.

1991

Crossing to Safety, Wallace Stegner. Sensitive and perceptive writer. We know the people Stegner wants us to know.

Ake: The Years of Childhood, Wole Soyinka. Lukewarm. Somewhat engaging story of a childhood, confusing place.

Composing a Life, Mary Catherine Bateson. Only relatively affluent women portrayed. Rather self-righteous and self-justifying.

Madame Bovary, Gustave Flaubert. Another woman with circumscribed choices, who has to die for being distinct, for doing what men do.

Anna Karenina, Leo Tolstoy. See *Madame Bovary*.

Their Eyes Were Watching God, Zora Neale Hurston. Dialect, gut-level speech and action. Deceptively simple. Had to read more Hurston.

A Midwife's Tale: The Life of Martha Ballard, Based on Her Diary 1785–1812, Laurel Thatcher Ulrich. The forming of America, with families as production units. Primarily work, more work, and death. Realization: at this same time, Mozart was composing in Vienna.

1992

Mrs. Caliban, Rachel Ingalls. A little book, a deep discussion. Is Larry real? Does it matter? Mysterious, frightening, unforgettable. Had to read more Ingalls.

Stones for Ibarra, Harriet Doerr. Intelligent and perceptive. A little too sparse to be entirely satisfying, but that's probably the point.

Mama Day, Gloria Naylor. Unusual. Told from varying points of view and it works. Magic and love. Had to read more Naylor.

House of Mirth, Edith Wharton. Wonderful portrayal of New York turn-of-the-century society and constraints on women. See *Madame Bovary* and *Anna Karenina*.

The Charterhouse of Parma, Stendhal. Love and politics. No one was much impressed.

Mrs. Dalloway, Virginia Woolf. One of Woolf's more accessible works. Discussion about Clarissa's happiness, sincerity, marriage. Yes.

As I Lay Dying, William Faulkner. Grim. Rough. Hopeless. Clearly a master.

Eichmann in Jerusalem, Hannah Arendt. Profound questions. Who is ultimately morally accountable?

Iron John, Robert Bly. Terrible scholarship. Sloppy writing. Almost humorous. The same old story—men, take charge, be "real" men, don't take any crap from women.

Women Respond to the Men's Movement, Kay Leigh Hagan, Editor. Anthology of responses from varied and articulate women. Diverse points of view. Lively discussion.

1993

A Thousand Acres, Jane Smiley. A brilliant undertaking. This one *deserved* the Pulitzer. We can never know the why of meanness, of blind ego; we can only witness the devastation it sows.

King Lear, Shakespeare. Read in conjunction with *A Thousand Acres*. Those who have taught *Lear* for years began to look at him and his daughters in a different light.

Angle of Repose, Wallace Stegner. The book our group is in the process of reading. Excellent already.

FEMINIST BOOK DISCUSSION GROUP BOOK LIST

Henrietta Bensussen with Sandra Miller
San Jose, California

1985

Another Mother Tongue, Judy Grahn
The Color Purple, Alice Walker
The Mists of Avalon, Marion Zimmer Bradley
Lesbian Nuns, Rosemary Curb and Nancy Manahan
Ancient Mirrors of Womanhood, Merlin Stone
Other Women, Lisa Alther
The Wanderground, Sally Gearhart

1986

Sisterhood Is Global, Robin Morgan
Zami: A New Spelling of My Name, Audre Lorde
The Kin of Ata Are Waiting for You, Dorothy Bryant
Choices, Nancey Toder
When God Was a Woman, Merlin Stone
A Reckoning, May Sarton

Goddesses in Everywoman, Jean Shinoda Bolin
The Ladies, Doris Grumbach
Sinking, Stealing, Jan Clausen
Gyn/Ecology, Mary Daly
Necessary Losses, Judith Viorst
Confessions of a Failed Southern Lady, Florence King

1987

Medicine Woman, Lynn Andrews
The House at Pelham Falls, Brenda Weather
Sisters of the Road, Barbara Wilson
Long Time Passing: Lives of Older Lesbians, Marcy Adelman
Elsa: I Come with My Songs, Elsa Gidlow
Confessions of Madame Psyche, Dorothy Bryant
The Handmaid's Tale, Margaret Atwood
Odd Girl Out, Ann Bannon
Going Out of Our Minds, Sonia Johnson
Their Eyes Were Watching God, Zora Neale Hurston
Soul Snatcher, Camarin Grae

1988

Memory Board, Jane Rule
Salt Eaters, Toni Cade Bambara
Unlit Lamp, Radclyffe Hall
Woman on the Edge of Time, Marge Piercy
Women and Nature, Susan Griffin
Beloved, Toni Morrison
Over the Hill: Reflections on Ageism Between Women,
   Baba Copper
Outrageous Acts and Everyday Rebellions, Gloria Steinem
The Chalice and the Blade, Riane Eisler
Mundane's World, Judy Grahn

1989

Through Other Eyes, Irene Zahava

Lesbian Couples, D. Merilee Clunis and G. Dorsey Green
The Woman Who Owned the Shadows, Paula Gunn Allen
Lesbian Ethics, Sarah Lucia Hoagland
All Good Women, Valerie Miner
Why Can't Sharon Kowalski Come Home, Karen Thompson
Womonseed, Sunlight
Daughters of Copper Woman, Anne Cameron
Wildfire, Sonia Johnson
Kindred, Octavia Butler
A Passion for Friends, Janice Raymond

1990

Cat's Eye, Margaret Atwood
The Price of Salt, Claire Morgan
Lesbian Love Stories, Irene Zahava
She Came in a Flash, Mary Wings
Borderlands/La Frontera, Gloria Anzaldua
The House of the Spirits, Isabel Allende
Cassandra, Christa Wolf
The Joy Luck Club, Amy Tan
The Female Man, Joanna Russ
A Restricted Country, Joan Nestle

1991

The Beet Queen, Louise Erdrich
The Temple of My Familiar, Alice Walker
This Bridge Called My Back, Cherrie Moraga and
   Gloria Anzaldua
Gaudi Afternoon, Barbara Wilson
A Little Original Sin, Millicent Dillon
Lesbians at Midlife, B. Sang, J. Warshow, and A. J. Smith
Final Session, Mary Morell
The Wounded Woman, Linda Leonard
Macho Sluts, Pat Califia
The Gilda Stories, Jewelle Gomez

The Ship That Sailed into the Living Room, Sonia Johnson
Trash, Dorothy Allison

1992

Woman of the 14th Moon, Dena Taylor and Amber Sumrall
The Search for Signs of Intelligent Life in the Universe,
   Jane Wagner
Fried Green Tomatoes at the Whistle Stop Cafe, Fannie Flagg
Margins, Terri de la Pena
Odd Girls and Twilight Lovers, Lillian Faderman
The Education of Harriet Hatfield, May Sarton
Closer to Home: Bisexuality and Feminism, Elizabeth Weise
Two-Bit Tango, Elizabeth Pincus

CLAREMONT PARK BOOK CLUB BOOK LIST

JoEllen Brean
Berkeley, California

The Moon by Whale Light, Diane Ackerman
Flowers in the Rain and Other Stories, Rosamunde Pilcher
Wilderness Tips, Margaret Atwood
Mansions of Limbo, Dominick Dunne
Food and Friends, Simone Beck
The Tokaido Road, Lucia St. Clare Robson
Matisse, Picasso and Miro As I Knew Them, Rosamond Bernier
Chasing the Monsoon, Alexander Fraser
Wild Swans, Jung Change
Wall to Wall from Beijing to Berlin, Mary Morris
A Terrible Liar, Hume Cronyn
Roman Blood, Steven Saylor
Murther and Walking Spirits, Robertson Davies
Money Culture, Michael Lewis
To the Scaffold, Carolly Erickson
Copper Crown, Lane Von Hertzen

The Divine Sarah: A Life of Sarah Bernhardt, Arthur Gold and
   Robert Fizdale
Parnell and the English Woman, Hugh Leonard
Night over Water, Ken Follett
Sign Posts, Walker Percy
Father Melancholy's Daughter, Gail Godwin
No More Minor Chords, Andre Previn
The Firm, John Grisham
Toujours Provence, Peter Mayle
PrairyErth (A Deep Map), William Least Heat-Moon
Family Money, Nina Bawdin
The Bug in the Martini Olive, Patricia Holt
On the Third Day, Piers Paul Read
Fireman's Fair, Josephine Humphreys
The Devil's Candy, Julie Salamon
The Good House, Jacobson, Silverstein, and Winslow
Saint Maybe, Anne Tyler
Courting Danger, Alice Marble
Dangerous Mourning, Anne Perry
How to Make an American Quilt, Whitney Otto
Den of Thieves, James B. Stewart
Catapault, Jim Paul
Russka, Edward Rutherford
The Kitchen God's Wife, Amy Tan
A Question of Character, Tom Reeves
Baghdad Without a Map and Other Misadventures in Arabia,
   Tony Horowitz
Searoad: Chronicles of Klatsand, Ursula LeGuin
I've Seen the Best, Joseph Alsop

BOOK
LIST

Mary Nell Bryant
Washington, D.C.

The Edible Woman, Margaret Atwood
Therese Raquin, Émile Zola
Democracy, Henry Adams
Mrs. Dalloway, Virginia Woolf
I Know Why the Caged Bird Sings, Maya Angelou
Age of Innocence, Edith Wharton
Autobiography of Alice B. Toklas, Gertrude Stein
The Warden, Anthony Trollope
Short Stories of John Cheever, John Cheever
Searching for Caleb, Anne Tyler
Vagabond, Colette
The Scarlet Pimpernel, Emmuska Orczy
All about Jeeves, P. G. Wodehouse
O Pioneers!, Willa Cather
Pale Horse, Pale Rider, Katherine Anne Porter
Small Changes, Marge Piercy

Dinner at the Homesick Restaurant, Anne Tyler
The Color Purple, Alice Walker
Aunt Julia and the Scriptwriter, Mario Vargas Llosa
In Memory of Old Jack, Wendell Berry
Innocents Abroad, Mark Twain
Excellent Women, Barbara Pym
Minor Characters, Joyce Johnson
The Master and Margarita, Mikhail Bulgakov
Happy to Be Here, Garrison Keillor
The Ambassadors, Henry James
Optimist's Daughter, Eudora Welty
Wide Sargasso Sea, Jean Rhys
Jane Eyre, Charlotte Brontë
A Mother and Two Daughters, Gail Godwin
Light in August, William Faulkner
Spring Snow, Yukio Mishima
Bartelby the Scrivener, Herman Melville
Book of Laughter and Forgetting, Milan Kundera
Blue Highways, William Least Heat-Moon
Out of Africa, Isak Dinesen
A Passage to India, E. M. Forster
During the Reign of the Queen of Persia, Joan Chase
Enormous Changes at the Last Minute, Grace Paley
Bright Lights, Big City, Jay McInerney
The Lost Honor of Katerina Blum, Heinrich Böll
West with the Night, Beryl Markham
Parallel Lives, Phyllis Rose
One Writer's Beginnings, Eudora Welty
The Reivers, William Faulkner
Desert Rose, Larry McMurtry
Mrs. Palfrey at the Claremont, Elizabeth Taylor
Swann's Way, Marcel Proust
Transit of Venus, Shirley Hazzard
Housekeeping, Marilynne Robinson
Down Among the Women, Fay Weldon

The Moviegoer, Walker Percy
Journal of a Solitude, May Sarton
A Room of One's Own, Virginia Woolf
The Sot-Weed Factor, John Barth
Fifth Business, Robertson Davies
Here to Get My Baby Out of Jail, Louise Shivers
Confessions of a Failed Southern Lady, Florence King
Hotel du Lac, Anita Brookner
Stones for Ibarra, Harriet Doerr
Accidental Tourist, Anne Tyler
House, Tracy Kidder
An Unsuitable Job for a Woman, P. D. James
Cannery Row, John Steinbeck
Lonesome Dove, Larry McMurtry
Villette, Charlotte Brontë
July's People, Nadine Gordimer
Last September, Elizabeth Bowen
The Power and the Glory, Graham Greene
The Old Forest and Other Stories, Peter Taylor
Monkeys, Susan Minot
What's Bred in the Bone, Robertson Davies
Song of Solomon, Toni Morrison
Death Comes for the Archbishop, Willa Cather
The Beet Queen, Louise Erdrich
Cakes and Ale, Somerset Maugham
Madame Bovary, Gustave Flaubert
The Scarlet Letter, Nathaniel Hawthorne
Family and Friends, Anita Brookner
Life and Death in Shanghai, Nien Cheng
A Yellow Raft in Blue Water, Michael Dorris
Miss Peabody's Inheritance, Elizabeth Jolley
Interview with a Vampire, Anne Rice
Of Love and Shadows, Isabel Allende
Dancing at the Rascal Fair, Ivan Doig
An American Childhood, Annie Dillard

Crossing to Safety, Wallace Stegner
Baltasar and Blimunda, Jose Saramago
Annie John, Jamaica Kincaid
Moon Tiger, Penelope Lively
Love in the Time of Cholera, Gabriel García Marquez
The Lover, Marguerite Duras
Mrs. Bridge, Evan S. Connell
Paris Trout, Peter Dexter
A Country Doctor, Sarah Orne Jewett
Dead Souls, Nikolai Gogol
Song of the Lark, Willa Cather
A Late Divorce, A. B. Yehoshua
Changing Places, David Lodge
The Whiteness of Bones, Susanna Moore
A Far Cry from Kensington, Muriel Spark
The Sheltering Sky, Paul Bowles
The Joy Luck Club, Amy Tan
Lost in Translation, Eva Hoffman
The Wanderer, Alain Fournier
The Road from Coorain, Jill Ker Conway
Remains of the Day, Kazuo Ishiguro
Pride and Prejudice, Jane Austen
The Lion, the Witch, and the Wardrobe, C. S. Lewis
All Hallow's Eve, Charles Williams
Beloved, Toni Morrison
Palace Walk, Naguib Mahfouz
Waterland, Graham Swift
Ake: The Years of Childhood, Wole Soyinka
The American Senator, Anthony Trollope
Friend of My Youth, Alice Munro
Angle of Repose, Wallace Stegner
The Diary of Helena Morley, translated by Elizabeth Bishop
Possession, A. S. Byatt
Widows' Adventure, Charles Dickinson
The Beautiful Mrs. Seidenman, Andrzej Szczypiorski

Cat's Eye, Margaret Atwood
Patrimony: A True Story, Philip Roth
The Bigamist's Daughter, Alice McDermott
Jasmine, Bharati Mukherjee
Ordinary Love and Good Will, Jane Smiley
The Kitchen God's Wife, Amy Tan
A Thousand Acres, Jane Smiley
A Life of Her Own: The Transformation of a Country Woman in 20th Century France, Emilie Curles
Flaubert's Parrot, Julian Barnes

SAMPLE BOOK LIST AND COMMENTS

Martha M. Bullen
Glen Ellyn, Illinois

I have been a member and leader of two book discussion groups for women—one with a local branch of the AAUW (American Association of University Women), and one with a chapter of FEMALE (Formerly Employed Mothers at the Leading Edge). Both groups primarily preferred to read women writers. We concentrated on fairly recent fiction, though we included a few nonfiction books in which members had expressed interest. The following list includes the books that provoked the most sparkling discussion and enjoyable reading.

Fiction

Stones for Ibarra, Harriet Doerr. A touching, lyrical novel about a small Mexican village where an American couple goes to retire, and the adjustments the couple must make during the course of the husband's fatal illness. The encounters between the Americans and the superstitious villagers are poignant and memorable. This book is a good way to encourage discussions of other cultures and what we have in common with them.

The Bean Trees, Barbara Kingsolver. Members enjoyed this quirky, funny, and touching look at how a young woman accidentally becomes the mother of an abandoned Native American child, and how that changes her life. It also offers a wonderful portrait of the modern southwest.

Family Pictures, Sue Miller. The story of a family with an autistic child, and how that child's differences affect all the members of the family. (Some groups might also enjoy this author's first novel, *The Good Mother*, which poses the question: Is a good mother someone who gives up everything for her child?)

How to Make an American Quilt, Whitney Otto. Wonderfully written descriptions of quilt-making are interspersed with poignant stories of the women in the quilting circle. An imaginative and involving first novel.

Quartet in Autumn, Barbara Pym. Sparked a lively discussion about aging and how to help those older people who don't want to be helped.

Object Lessons, Anna Quindlen. This absorbing first novel by the *New York Times* Pulitzer Prize–winning columnist is about a young Italian-American girl's coming of age. It led to a good discussion about growing into womanhood in the midst of a contentious family.

Me and My Baby View the Eclipse, Lee Smith. Light, funny, short stories about a motley collection of southerners, their daily lives, and their dreams.

The Joy Luck Club, Amy Tan. A wonderful, heartbreaking look at mother-daughter relationships, as well as a crash course in recent Chinese history. Very involving even for women whose only contact with China is their local Chinese restaurant.

Dinner at the Homesick Restaurant, Anne Tyler. A marvelous story set around a family's longing for communion, and their inability to share a simple dinner together without one of the members storming off in anger. One of Tyler's finest books, and a great starting point for discussions on family dynamics.

Earthly Possessions, Anne Tyler. An early Tyler novel, this one involves a young mother of two who is kidnapped by a bank robber one morning as she prepares to leave her husband. Despite the plot summary, it's not a thriller. Instead, it's a wise look at the meaning of family (yet again!) and possessions in our lives, and the conflict between the desire for safety and escape.

The Color Purple, Alice Walker. This was not a success at our first book group. Most of the middle-aged, financially comfortable, suburban women who attended the meeting refused to believe that this book had any resemblance to real life. They kept saying, "These things just don't happen!" It's a great book for those willing to confront and explore the issues of racism and child abuse.

Nonfiction

Among Sisters, Susan Cahill. An in-depth look at the fundamental bond between sisters. The women in the group enjoyed sharing their own stories on this topic.

Between Women: Love, Competition, and Envy in Women's Friendships, Louise Eichenbaum and Susi Orbach. An eye-opening discussion of the rivalry and anger that often lurk behind the pleasant facades of women's friendships. The authors argue that women should start being honest with each other instead of adding to the illusion that no conflict exists. Group members found it thought-provoking and generally true to their experiences.

Prisoners of Men's Dreams, Suzanne Gordon. A serious study of the reasons that caregiving is undervalued in today's society. Discusses one of the failures of the women's movement—that women decided to emulate men and strive for success in the workplace instead of using their collective power to make the work world more family-friendly. Lots of meat for discussion here.

Parallel Lives, Phyllis Rose. A marvelous description of the marriages of five prominent Victorian writers: John Ruskin, Thomas Carlyle, John Stuart Mill, Charles Dickens, and George Eliot. Very compelling look at the idea of marriage and the balance of power within it. Most of the issues she raises are still common concerns today. We had one of our most rousing discussions about this book.

Women Together, Women Alone, Anita Shreve. Interesting look at the women's consciousness raising movement of the 1960s and its legacy in recent times. Offers some ideas for resurrecting these groups, and explains why they helped change American society.

BOOK
LIST

Ann Christophersen
Chicago, Illinois

I've grouped the books we've read into three categories: hits, mixed, and unmemorable. To clarify my book list, almost all the books we read are "good" books. My rating of them is based on two things: that people *liked* the book *and* that we had an inspired discussion for the hits; that some of the group liked the book, while others didn't and we had decent discussion for the books in the mixed category; or that the book was OK, but we had an uninspired discussion for those books I've listed as unmemorable. In the case of the unmemorables, I think part of the trouble was we didn't always know *how* to discuss the book, which means a book's inclusion in either the mixed or unmemorable category could be more a reflection on our group than on the book's quality.

Hits

The Twilight Years, Sawaki Ariyoshi
The Age of Grief and *A Thousand Acres*, Jane Smiley
The Passion, Jeanette Winterson

Woman Hollering Creek, Sandra Cisneros
Odd Girls and Twilight Lovers, Lillian Faderman
The Revolution of Little Girls, Blanche McCrary Boyd
Obscene Gestures for Women, Janet Kauffman
Friend of My Youth, Alice Munro
Middleman and Other Stories and *Jasmine*, Bharati Mukherjee
Before and After, Rosellen Brown
Woman at Point Zero, Nawal el-Saadawi
Road from Coorain, Jill Ker Conway
Kindred, Octavia Butler
At Weddings and Wakes, Alice McDermott
Age of Innocence, Edith Wharton
Possession, A. S. Byatt
Beloved, Toni Morrison
Stone Angel, Margaret Laurence
Jane Eyre, Charlotte Brontë

Mixed

Mrs. Caliban and *Be My Guest*, Rachel Ingalls
Fifth Child, Doris Lessing
Jazz, Toni Morrison
Sugar Mothers, Elizabeth Jolley
AIDS and Its Metaphors and *Against Interpretation*,
   Susan Sontag
Joy Luck Club, Amy Tan
Breathing Lessons, Anne Tyler
The Woman Who Wasn't All There, Paula Sharp
Cat's Eye, Margaret Atwood
Creation of Patriarchy, Gerda Lerner
In a Different Voice, Carol Gilligan
Women's Ways of Knowing, Mary Field Belenky, et al.
Cities on a Hill, Frances FitzGerald
Time's Power, Adrienne Rich
Blue Taxis, Eileen Drew
Spider Woman's Granddaughters, Paula Gunn Allen

Backlash, Susan Faludi
Sarah Canary, Karen Joy Fowler
Optimist's Daughter, Eudora Welty
Reinventing Home, Laurie Abraham, et al.
Family Pictures, Sue Miller
Balancing Acts and *Leaving Brooklyn*, Lynne Sharon Schwartz
All-Bright Court, Connie Porter

Unmemorable

Feminism Unmodified, Catharine MacKinnon
Composing a Life, Mary Catherine Bateson
Writing a Woman's Life, Carolyn Heilbrun
Really Reading Gertrude Stein, Judy Grahn

BEMIDJI BOOK CLUB READING LIST

Alice V. Collins
Bemidji, Minnesota

1985

Wuthering Heights, Emily Brontë
Growing Up, Russell Baker
Lutefisk Ghetto, Art Lee
Love and War, John Jakes

1986

Hunt for Red October, Tom Clancy
Iacocca, Lee Iacocca
A Distant Mirror, Barbara Tuchman
Ironweed, William Kennedy
Walking Drum, Louis L'Amour
The Agony and the Ecstasy, Irving Stone
On Wings of Eagles, Ken Follett
The Diary of a Provincial Lady, E. M. Dellifield
The Adventures of Huckleberry Finn, Mark Twain

1987

Strange Encounters, Mike Wallace
The Haj, Leon Uris
Nutcracker, Shana Alexander
Common Ground, Anthony Lucas
The Beans of Egypt, Maine, Carolyn Chute

1988

Pride and Prejudice, Jane Austen
The Red and the Black, Stendahl
Grand Opening, Jon Hassler
Silent Partner, Judith Greber

1989

Taming of the Shrew, Shakespeare
Hatchet, Gary Paulsen
Walden, Henry David Thoreau
Vanity Fair, William Makepeace Thackeray
The Accidental Tourist, Anne Tyler
Les Miserables, Victor Hugo
Cold Sassy Tree, Olive Ann Burns
Lonesome Dove, Larry McMurtry
84, Charing Cross Road, Helene Hanff

1990

Killing Time in St. Cloud, Judith Guest
Spring Moon, Betty Bao Lord
Crossing to Safety, Wallace Stegner
Love Medicine, Louise Erdrich
Love in the Time of Cholera, Gabriel García Marquez
Indian Givers, Jack Weatherford
The Sun Also Rises, Ernest Hemingway
Type Talk, Otto Kroeger

1991

Jubilee, Margaret Walker
Billy Bathgate, E. L. Doctorow
The Big Rock Candy Mountain, Wallace Stegner
Once Upon a Time on the Banks, Cathie Pelletier
Pilgrim at Tinker Creek, Annie Dillard
A River Runs Through It, Norman MacLean
When Rabbit Howls, Trudy Chase
The Power and the Glory, Graham Greene
A Cup of Christmas Tea, Tom Hegg

1992

Necessity of Empty Spaces, Paul Gruchow
Death in Venice, Thomas Mann
Rabbit Run, John Updike
Ashana, E. P. Roesch
A Is for Alibi, Sue Grafton
Oldest Living Confederate Widow Tells All, Allan Gurganus
Walking Across Egypt, Clyde Edgerton
Mark of the Maker, Tom Hegg
Secret Garden, Frances Hodgson Burnett

BOOK
LIST

Cindra Halm
Minneapolis, Minnesota

Their Eyes Were Watching God, Zora Neale Hurston
Disturbance in the Field, Lynne Sharon Schwartz
Nine Stories, J. D. Salinger
The Grapes of Wrath, John Steinbeck
Anna Karenina, Leo Tolstoy
Wise Blood, Flannery O'Connor
The Book of Laughter and Forgetting, Milan Kundera
Illness as Metaphor, Susan Sontag
Lonesome Dove, Larry McMurtry
Love in the Time of Cholera, Gabriel García Marquez
The Hamlet, William Faulkner
Typee, Herman Melville
Eva Luna, Isabel Allende
Sentimental Education, Gustave Flaubert
Feeding the Eagles, Paulette Bates Alden
Annie John, Jamaica Kincaid

The Mambo Kings Play Songs of Love, Oscar Hijuelos
Flaubert's Parrot, Julian Barnes
After the Banquet, Yukio Mishima
Lolita, Vladimir Nabokov
The Loved One, Evelyn Waugh
Daughters, Paule Marshall

POETRY
LIST

Peggy Heinrich
Westport, Connecticut

Some of our favorite contemporary poets have been Elizabeth Bishop, Robert Bly, Lucille Clifton, Nikki Giovanni, Stanley Kunitz, Li-Young Lee, Sharon Olds, Mary Oliver, Theodore Roethke, Gary Snyder, Charles Simic, William Stafford, and Derek Walcott.

Others we've enjoyed are Eavan Boland, Billy Collins, Stephen Dunn, Louise Erdrich, Tess Gallagher, Seamus Heaney, Maxine Kumin, Derek Mahon, Stephen Mitchell, Richard Wilbur, and James Wright.

We've been divided about John Ashbery, Raymond Carver, Allen Ginsberg, Dana Gioia, Brad Leithauser, Cynthia Macdonald, James Merrill, Alicia Ostriker, Adrienne Rich, Anne Sexton, Mark Strand, and Mona Van Duyn.

Although translated poetry loses its original flavor, we haven't overlooked wonderful foreign poets such as Yehuda Amichai, C. P. Cavafy, Czeslaw Milosz, Pablo Neruda, and Octavio Paz.

Nor have we ignored the long-established poets we first met in school, such as Browning, Dickinson, Keats, Shelley, Wordsworth, and Whitman, or the bright lights of the twentieth century, Auden, Eliot, Rilke, Yeats, Hart Crane, Dylan Thomas, Wallace Stevens, and William Carlos Williams.

BOOK
LIST

Stephen A. Huth
Oak Park, Illinois

The Harvey Avenue Book Club (it doesn't really have a name, but most of the original members lived on the 200 block of south Harvey) began partially because all but one of the founding members had an infant, and a neighborhood book club gave us a chance to get out of the house. The book club is now twelve years old, with twelve members (six couples)—six of the members are original.

We meet about eight times a year. We move from house to house. The person who is host picks the book. Almost without exception, we've read contemporary books. Discussions, which are always followed by dessert and coffee, are very informal. Because we are all neighbors, we often spend time catching up on neighborhood gossip.

Below is a mostly complete list of the books we have read in the past twelve years. Half a dozen or so titles may be missing (we don't keep records). If I was better organized and had started sooner, I could tell you stories of the chocolate and the kitty litter, and the Christmas Carol that wasn't—maybe in another life.

The Accidental Tourist, Anne Tyler
Adventures of Augie March, Saul Bellow
At Risk, Alice Hoffman
The Beans of Egypt, Maine, Carolyn Chute
The Beet Queen, Louise Erdrich
Beloved, Toni Morrison
The Bluest Eye, Toni Morrison
The Bonfire of the Vanities, Tom Wolfe
Book of Daniel, E. L. Doctorow
Braided Lives, Marge Piercy
Breathing Lessons, Anne Tyler
Bright Lights, Big City, Jay McInerney
Burger's Daughter, Nadine Gordimer
Call It Sleep, Philip Roth
A Canticle for Liebowitz, Walter Miller
China Men, Maxine Hong Kingston
Cities on a Hill, Frances FitzGerald
Clan of the Cave Bear, Jean Auel
The Color Purple, Alice Walker
Confederacy of Dunces, John Kennedy Toole
Confidence Man, Herman Melville
Crows, Charles Dickinson
Devil's Stocking, Nelson Algren
Dinner at the Homesick Restaurant, Anne Tyler
A Fan's Notes, Frederick Exley
Far Pavilions, M. M. Kaye
From Beirut to Jerusalem, Thomas Friedman
God Knows and *Good As Gold*, Joseph Heller
Growing Up, Russell Baker
The Handmaid's Tale, Margaret Atwood
Hocus Pocus, Kurt Vonnegut
I Know Why the Caged Bird Sings, Maya Angelou

The Ice Age, Margaret Drabble
Ironweed, William Kennedy
Jefferson, Fawn McKay Brodie
The Joy Luck Club, Amy Tan
The Keepers of the House, Shirley Grau
Libra, Don DeLillo
Life and Death in Shanghai, Nien Cheng
Lincoln, Gore Vidal
Linden Hills, Gloria Naylor
Loon Lake, E. L. Doctorow
Love Medicine, Louise Erdrich
Manticore, Robertson Davies
Midnight's Children, Salman Rushdie
The Mists of Avalon, Marion Zimmer Bradley
More Die of Heartbreak, Saul Bellow
Mrs. Caliban, Rachel Ingalls
The Name of the Rose, Umberto Eco
The Natural, Bernard Malumud
On the Beach, Neville Chute
One Hundred Years of Solitude, Gabriel García Marquez
Oral History, Lee Smith
Out of Africa, Isak Dinesen
Paco's Story, Larry Heinemann
Palace Walk, Naguib Mahfouz
A Prayer for Owen Meany, John Irving
Ragtime, E. L. Doctorow
Remains of the Day, Kazuo Ishiguro
Roger's Version, John Updike
Schindler's List, Thomas Keneally
The Screwtape Letters, C. S. Lewis
Setting Free the Bears, John Irving
The Seven Per Cent Solution, Nicholas Meyer
Small Is Beautiful, E. F. Schumacher
Son of the Morning Star, Evan Connell
Sophie's Choice, William Styron

Tar Baby, Toni Morrison
There Are No Children Here, Alex Kotlowitz
Trial of Socrates, I. F. Stone
The Unbearable Lightness of Being, Milan Kundera
Waltz in Marathon, Charles Dickinson
Warday, Whitley Streiber and James Kunetka
The Woman Warrior, Maxine Hong Kinston
Welcome to Hard Times, E. L. Doctorow
West with the Night, Beryl Markham
What's Bred in the Bones, Robertson Davies
Widows' Adventure and *With or Without*, Charles Dickinson
The World According to Garp, John Irving
A Yellow Raft in Blue Water, Michael Dorris

BARNES & NOBLE ADULT BOOK CLUB SUGGESTED READINGS

Vicki Katz
Deerfield, Illinois

General Fiction

Mating, Norman Rush
Daughters, Paule Marshall
Typical American, Gish Jen
Time's Arrow, Martin Amis
Isaac and His Devils, Fernanda Eberstadt
Bronze Mirror, Jeanne Larsen
Copper Crown, Lane von Herzen
Animal Dreams, Barbara Kingsolver
The Sweet Hereafter, Russell Banks
Mariette in Ecstasy, Ron Hansen
Possession, A. S. Byatt
Cat's Eye and *The Handmaid's Tale*, Margaret Atwood
Disappearing Acts, Terry McMillan
Heart of Darkness, Joseph Conrad
A Thousand Acres, Jane Smiley

The Kitchen God's Wife and *The Joy Luck Club*, Amy Tan
A Summons to Memphis, Peter Taylor

Nonfiction

Backlash, Susan Faludi
You Just Don't Understand, Deborah Tannen

Arthurian Legends

The Mists of Avalon, Marion Zimmer Bradley
Arthur Rex, Thomas Berger
The Once and Future King, T. H. White

It's a Classical Gas!

Women in Love, D. H. Lawrence
The Europeans, Henry James
For Whom the Bell Tolls, Ernest Hemingway
Frankenstein, Mary Shelley
Moll Flanders, Daniel Defoe
Far from the Madding Crowd, Thomas Hardy
Howards End, E. M. Forster
Tender Is the Night, F. Scott Fitzgerald
The Call of the Wild, Jack London
Jane Eyre, Charlotte Brontë
The Red Badge of Courage, Stephen Crane
Great Expectations, Charles Dickens
A Room of One's Own, Virginia Woolf
Silas Marner, George Eliot
A Good Man Is Hard to Find, Flannery O'Connor
The Optimist's Daughter, Eudora Welty
The Bell Jar, Sylvia Plath
Pride and Prejudice, Jane Austen
The Scarlet Letter, Nathaniel Hawthorne
The Picture of Dorian Gray, Oscar Wilde

AN INCOMPLETE READING LIST FROM THE DETROIT FEMINIST READING GROUP

Susan Knoppow
Royal Oak, Michigan

Women of Ideas and What Men Have Done to Them,
  Dale Spender
An Atlas of the Difficult World, Adrienne Rich
Meme Santerre, Serge Grafteaux
Women Respond to the Men's Movement, Kay Leigh Hagan, ed.
Summer People, Marge Piercy
Fried Green Tomatoes at the Whistle Stop Cafe, Fannie Flagg
The Women's History of the World, Rosalind Miles
Monkeys, Susan Minot
Homeland and *Animal Dreams,* Barbara Kingsolver
Backlash, Susan Faludi
The Four-Gated City, Doris Lessing
A Room of One's Own, Virginia Woolf
The Yellow Wallpaper, Charlotte Perkins Gilman
John Dollar, Marianne Wiggins
Cat's Eye and *The Handmaid's Tale,* Margaret Atwood
Women of Deh Koh, Erika Friedl
Always Coming Home, Ursula K. LeGuin

"WRITERS ON READING" SELECTIONS

F. R. Lewis
Albany, New York

Bartelby the Scrivener, Herman Melville
House of Mirth, Edith Wharton
Angels, Denis Johnson
Summons to Memphis, Peter Taylor
The Beans of Egypt, Maine (stimulated lots of discussion),
   Carolyn Chute
Growing Up Rich, Anne Bernays
The Barracks Thief and selected stories, Tobias Wolff
The Bluest Eye (everyone loved it), Toni Morrison
World's Fair, E. L. Doctorow
Country of the Pointed Firs (a surprise), Sarah Orne Jewett
Big Foot Dreams, Francine Prose
So Long, See You Tomorrow, William Maxwell
Going After Cacciato, Tim O'Brien
Death Comes for the Archbishop, Willa Cather
That Night, Alice McDermott

Housekeeping (a favorite), Marilynne Robinson
The Accidental Tourist, Anne Tyler
Burger's Daughter, Nadine Gordimer
Sanctuary, William Faulkner
My Brilliant Career, Miles Franklin
Perfume, Patrick Suskind
Wise Blood, Flannery O'Connor
Stones for Ibarra, Harriet Doerr
Enormous Changes at the Last Minute, Grace Paley
The Unbearable Lightness of Being, Milan Kundera
Angle of Repose (a discovery), Wallace Stegner
Tess of the d'Urbervilles, Thomas Hardy
Fifth Business (we discovered a writer we loved),
    Robertson Davies
Fifth Column and Four Stories of the Spanish Civil War,
    Ernest Hemingway
The Good Soldier, Ford Madox Ford
The Best Cellar, Charles Goodrum
Nature's End, Whitley Streiber and James Kunetka
Love Medicine, Louise Erdrich
Cat's Eye (loved it), Margaret Atwood
The Moviegoer (great), Walker Percy
To the Lighthouse, Virginia Woolf
The Quest for Christa T. (rough going), Christa Wolf
The Sound of the Mountain, Yasunari Kawabata
Guerillas, V. S. Naipaul
Dexterity (a writer with local connections), Douglas Bauer
Spartina, John Casey
Cora Fry, Rosellen Brown
The Bottom of the River, Jamaica Kincaid
The Mill on the Floss, George Eliot
The Power and the Glory, Graham Greene
The Counterlife, Philip Roth
Things Fall Apart, Chinua Achebe
The Heidi Chronicles, Wendy Wasserstein

A Moon for the Misbegotten and *Long Day's Journey Into Night*,
  Eugene O'Neill
The Wind in the Willows (difficult to discuss),
  Kenneth Grahame
Selected Stories, Andre Dubus
Good Behavior, Molly Keane
The Second Shift, Arlie Hochschild
Panama, Thomas McGuane
Country Girls Trilogy, Edna O'Brien
An Artist of the Floating World, Kazuo Ishiguro
The Passion (challenging), Jeanette Winterson
The Education of Little Tree, Forrest Carter
An American Tragedy, Theodore Dreiser
Song of Solomon, Toni Morrison
Home Economics, Wendell Berry
In Limestone Country, Scott Russell Sanders
Iron Heel, Jack London
Their Eyes Were Watching God, Zora Neale Hurston
The Things They Carried, Tim O'Brien
A River Runs Through It, Norman MacLean
An American Childhood, Annie Dillard

BOOK LIST

Sara Manewith
Chicago, Illinois

Beauty Secrets, Wendy Chapkis
Animal Dreams, Barbara Kingsolver
Lucy, Jamaica Kincaid
The Bone People, Keri Hulme
A Yellow Raft in Blue Water, Michael Dorris
Frida: A Biography of Frida Kahlo, Hayden Herrera
Breathing Lessons, Anne Tyler
Invisible Man, Ralph Ellison
Good Girls/Bad Girls, Laurie Bell, ed.
Nora: A Biography of Nora Joyce, Brenda Maddox
West with the Night, Beryl Markham
A Room of One's Own, Virginia Woolf
Of Woman Born, Adrienne Rich
The House of the Spirits, Isabel Allende
The Beet Queen, Louise Erdrich
The Handmaid's Tale, Margaret Atwood

Disturbances in the Field, Lynne Sharon Schwartz
August, Judith Rossner
The Good Mother, Sue Miller
Life and Death in Shanghai, Nien Cheng
Beloved, Toni Morrison
Burger's Daughter, Nadine Gordimer
Cat's Eye, Margaret Atwood
The Joy Luck Club, Amy Tan
Gone to Soldiers, Marge Piercy
When Heaven and Earth Changed Places, Le Ly Hayslip
An American Childhood, Annie Dillard
The Road from Coorain, Jill Ker Conway
Ripening, Meridel LeSueur
Love in the Time of Cholera, Gabriel García Marquez
Temple of My Familiar, Alice Walker
Geek Love, Katherine Dunn
The Mambo Kings Play Songs of Love, Oscar Hijuelos
The Vagabond, Colette
The Fifth Child, Doris Lessing
House on Mango Street, Sandra Cisneros
Backlash, Susan Faludi
There Are No Children Here, Alex Kotlowitz
Woman Hollering Creek, Sandra Cisneros

BOOK
LIST

Curt Matthews,
Evanston, Illinois

1979

Symposium, Plato
Eichmann in Jerusalem, Hannah Arendt
Persuasion, Jane Austen
Introductory Essays, Sigmund Freud
Swann's Way, Marcel Proust
Lying, Sissela Bok
The White Hotel, D. M. Thomas
Father and Son, Edmund Gosse
Fathers and Sons, Ivan Turgenev
A House for Mr. Biswas, V. S. Naipaul
Lives of a Cell, Lewis Thomas

1980

Small House at Allington, Anthony Trollope
Confessions, Jean Jacques Rousseau

The Odyssey, Homer
Stories, Doris Lessing
A Bend in the River, V. S. Naipaul
Is There No Place on Earth for Me?, Susan Sheehan
Drawing on the Right Side of the Brain, Betty Edwards
Art and Illusion, E. H. Gombrich
The Structure of Scientific Revolutions, Thomas Kuhn
Les Liaisons Dangereuses, Pierre Choderlos de Laclos

1981

Civilization and Its Discontents, Sigmund Freud
Eminent Victorians, Lytton Strachey
Brideshead Revisited, Evelyn Waugh
Burger's Daughter, Nadine Gordimer
The Fate of the Earth, Jonathan Schell
Montaillou, Emmanuel Le Roy Ladurie
Rabbit Is Rich, John Updike
Loving, Henry Green
In a Budding Grove, Marcel Proust
Sonnets, Shakespeare

1982

The Last Chronicle of Barset, Anthony Trollope
Selected Stories, V. S. Pritchett
The Sea, the Sea, Iris Murdoch
The Mismeasure of Man, Stephen Jay Gould
War and Peace, Leo Tolstoy
Excellent Women, Barbara Pym
Confederacy of Dunces, John Kennedy Toole
Portrait of a Lady, Henry James

1983

Cranopios and Famas, Julio Cortazar
Wide Sargasso Sea, Jean Rhys
Gospels, Bible

As I Lay Dying and *Absalom, Absalom!*, William Faulkner
A Chronicle of a Death Foretold, Gabriel Garcia Marquez
Trouble in the Freud Archives, Janet Malcolm
The Aeneid, Virgil
Collected Poems, William Butler Yeats

1984

The Name of the Rose, Umberto Eco
The Heart of Midlothian, Sir Walter Scott
This Hallowed Ground, Bruce Catton
Adam Bede, George Eliot
Parallel Lives, Phyllis Rose
The Great Cat Massacre, Robert Darnton
The Good Soldier, Ford Madox Ford
The Sun Also Rises, Ernest Hemingway
What Maisie Knew, Henry James

1985

Purity and Danger, Mary Douglas
The Return of Martin Guerre, Natalie Zemon Davis
Collected Poems, Wallace Stevens
A Sense of Order, E. H. Gombrich
Man and the Natural World, Keith Thomas
Hippolytus, Euripides
Phaedra, Jean Racine
The Witches of Eastwick, John Updike
Home Before Dark, Susan Cheever
Kiss of the Spider Woman, Manuel Puig

1986

The Flanders Road, Claude Simon
A Late Divorce, Abraham Yehoshua
Uncle Vanya, Anton Chekhov
Bible and Sword, Barbara Tuchman
The Beans of Egypt, Maine, Carolyn Chute

Patterns of Culture, Ruth Benedict
Awakenings, Oliver Sacks

1987

Ficciones, Jorge Luis Borges
The History of an Idea, Allan Hoffman
A Lesser Life, Sylvia Hewitt
Presumed Innocent, Scott Turow
The Closing of the American Mind, Allan Bloom
Selected Short Stories, Franz Kafka
The Nightmare of Reason, Ernst Pawel

1988

Madwoman in the Attic, Sandra M. Gilbert
West with the Night, Beryl Markham
Reindeer Moon, Elizabeth Marshall Thomas
Anna Karenina, Leo Tolstoy
The Double Helix, James Watson
The Counterlife, Philip Roth
The Way We Live Now, Anthony Trollope

1989

Imagining Argentina, Lawrence Thornton
The Middle of My Tether, Joseph Epstein
The Songlines, Bruce Chatwin
Fatal Shore, Robert Hughes
Discipline and Punish, Michel Foucault
The Misanthrope, Moliere

1990

Ishi in Two Worlds, Theodora Kroeber
Tracks, Louise Erdrich
Brothers and Keepers, John Edgar Wideman
Lincoln-Douglas Debates
Memoirs of Hadrian, Marguerite Yourcenar

Christianity, Social Tolerance, and Homosexuality, John Boswell
Remains of the Day, Kazuo Ishiguro

1991

Even Cowgirls Get the Blues, Tom Robbins
Flights of Passage, Samuel Lynn Hynes
Case Studies, Sigmund Freud
From Beirut to Jerusalem, Thomas Friedman
Patrimony, Philip Roth
The Armada, Garrett Mattingly
Baron in the Trees, Italo Calvino
You Just Don't Understand, Deborah Tannen

1992

Culture and Anomie, Christopher Herbert
Emma, Jane Austen
The Nun, Diderot
The Varieties of Religious Experience, William James
Little Dorrit, Charles Dickens
Foe, J. M. Coetzee
A Midwife's Tale, Laurel Ulrich Thatcher
Making Sex, Thomas Laqueur
The Secret History, Donna Tartt
The Character of Physical Law, Richard Phillips Feynman

TENTH ANNIVERSARY BOOK LIST

Debby Mayer
New York City

1978

Molloy, Samuel Beckett
Robert Lowell poems
Invisible Cities, Italo Calvino
Jude the Obscure, Thomas Hardy
Under the Volcano, Malcolm Lowry
Thirteen Stories, Eudora Welty
Philip Larkin poems
Billiards at Half-Past Nine, Heinrich Böll
The Secret Agent, Joseph Conrad
Henrik Ibsen plays
James Merrill poems

1979

To the Lighthouse and *Waves*, Virginia Woolf
Life of Johnson, James Boswell
The Princess Casamassima, Henry James

Madame Bovary, Gustave Flaubert
Peter Handke novellas
Walden, Henry David Thoreau
Elizabeth Bishop poems
Dubliners, James Joyce
Tropic of Cancer, Henry Miller
Down and Out in Paris and London and *Road to Wigan Pier*,
  George Orwell
The Origin of the Species, Charles Darwin

1980

About Looking, John Berger
Howards End, E. M. Forster
Civilization and Its Discontents, Sigmund Freud
The House of Mirth, Edith Wharton
The Executioner's Song, Norman Mailer
Will You Please Be Quiet, Please?, Raymond Carver
Adam Bede, George Eliot
The Spy Who Came in from the Cold, John LeCarre
The Heart Is a Lonely Hunter, Carson McCullers
Flanner O'Connor stories
Anton Chekhov stories
King Lear, Shakespeare

1981

Robert Frost poems
Desperate Characters, Paula Fox
The Zero-Sum Society, Lester Thurow
In a Free State, V. S. Naipaul
Mansfield Park, Jane Austen
Memoirs of Hadrian, Marguerite Yourcenar
The White Album, Joan Didion
The Outermost House, Henry Beston
The Adventures of Huckleberry Finn, Mark Twain
How German Is It?, Walter Abish

1982

Appointment in Samarra, John O'Hara
The Great War and Modern Memory, Paul Fussell
A Flag for Sunrise, Robert Stone
Nostromo, Joseph Conrad
Riddley Walker, Russell Hoban
Tobacco Road, Erskine Caldwell
Labyrinths, Jorge Luis Borges
The Education of Henry Adams, Henry Adams
Autumn of the Patriarch, Gabriel García Marquez
Lucky Jim, Kingsley Amis

1983

Fifth Business, Robertson Davies
The Color Purple, Alice Walker
The Dancing Wu-Li Masters, Gary Zukav
Literary Theory, Terry Eagleton
Our Mutual Friend, Charles Dickens
London Embassy, Paul Theroux
Billy Phelan's Greatest Game, William Kennedy

1984

A Hero of Our Time, Mikhail Lermontov
Ellis Island, Mark Helprin
The Prelude, William Wordsworth
Jewel in the Crown, Paul Scott
Moby-Dick, Herman Melville
Selected Poems, Seamus Heaney
Parallel Lives, Phyllis Rose
The Age of Reason, Jean-Paul Sartre
Machine Dreams, Jayne Anne Phillips

1985

Kiss of the Spider Woman, Manuel Puig

July's People, Nadine Gordimer
The Silence, Shusaku Endo
Death of an Expert Witness, P. D. James
Two Women, Alberto Moravia
Crash, J. G. Ballard
Continental Drift, Russell Banks
The Good Soldier, Ford Madox Ford
A River Runs Through It, Norman MacLean

1986

The Death of Ivan Ilych, Leo Tolstoy
Man's Fate, Andre Malraux
The Scarlet Letter, Nathaniel Hawthorne
The Assault, Henry Mulisch
Flaubert's Parrot, Julian Barnes
Keat's Odes, Helen Hennessy Vendler
The Sweet Dove Died, Barbara Pym
Contemporary American Essays, Maureen Howard, ed.
Mohawk, Richard Russo
Collected Stories, Peter Taylor
The Mantle of the Prophet, Roy P. Mottahedeh

1987

The Plague, Albert Camus
The Group, Mary McCarthy
Wallace Stevens poems
A Handful of Dust, Evelyn Waugh
Time Will Darken It, William Maxwell
The Periodic Table, Primo Levi
Foxybaby, Elizabeth Jolley
Robert Burns poems
The House of the Spirits, Isabel Allende
The Decameron, Giovanni Boccacio
Their Eyes Were Watching God, Zora Neale Hurston

BOOK LIST

Marilyn Monaco-Han
Brooklyn, New York

Anywhere but Here, Mona Simpson
Middlemarch, George Eliot
A Summons to Memphis, Peter Taylor
My Antonia, Willa Cather
Beloved, Toni Morrison
Billy Bathgate, E. L. Doctorow
Remains of the Day, Kazuo Ishiguro
A Tale of Two Cities, Charles Dickens
Mansfield Park, Jane Austen
The Bonfire of the Vanities, Tom Wolfe
Charm School, Nelson DeMille
Oranges Are Not the Only Fruit, Jeanette Winterson
Counterlife, Philip Roth
The Awakening, Kate Chopin
Lives and Loves of a She Devil, Fay Weldon
Earth Sea Trilogy, Ursula K. LeGuin

Aunt Julia and the Scriptwriter, Mario Vargas Llosa
The Leopard, Giuseppe di Lampedusa
Writing a Woman's Life, Carolyn Heilbrun
Gaudy Night, Dorothy Sayers
War and Peace, Leo Tolstoy
Jude the Obscure, Thomas Hardy
The House of the Spirits, Isabel Allende
Woman on the Edge of Time, Marge Piercy
Fifth Business, Robertson Davies
Midnight's Children, Salman Rushdie
Mrs. Bridge, Evan S. Connell
Cakes and Ale, Somerset Maugham
As I Lay Dying, William Faulkner
Bleak House, Charles Dickens
The Good Terrorist, Doris Lessing
Foreign Affairs, Alison Lurie
The Bigamist's Daughter, Alice McDermott
The Temple of My Familiar, Alice Walker
Frankenstein, Mary Shelley
Love Medicine, Louise Erdrich
Fair and Tender Ladies, Lee Smith
To Kill a Mockingbird, Harper Lee
To the Lighthouse, Virginia Woolf
The Age of Grief, Jane Smiley
The Assault, Harry Mulisch
The Greater Trumps, Charles Williams
Time and Again, Jack Finney
A Virtuous Woman, Kay Gibbons
Possession, A. S. Byatt
Animal Dreams, Barbara Kingsolver
The Razor's Edge, Somerset Maugham
Accident, Christa Wolf
At Play in the Fields of the Lord, Peter Matthiessen
The Adventures of Huckleberry Finn, Mark Twain
Oscar and Lucinda, Peter Carey

Cheri and *The Vagabond*, Colette
Losing Battles, Eudora Welty
Aquamarine, Carol Anshaw
All Men Are Mortal, Simone de Beauvoir
A Thousand Acres, Jane Smiley
A Secret History, Donna Tartt
The Age of Innocence, Edith Wharton
Lady Chatterley's Lover, D. H. Lawrence

BOOK
LIST

Stephanie Patterson
Philadelphia, Pennsylvania

1989

Eva Luna, Isabel Allende. Big disappointment.

1990

Memory Board, Jane Rule. Good intentions, but conflicts resolved too easily.

Cat's Eye, Margaret Atwood. A wonderful book. The defining moment for our book group.

This Boy's Life: A Memoir, Tobias Wolff. Excellent. Read it in tandem with his brother Geoffrey's book, *The Duke of Deception*.

Ship of Fools, Katherine Anne Porter. Hated it. I'm glad she wrote short stories.

Angels on Toast, Dawn Powell. An acquired taste. Generally not well received by our group.

The Joy Luck Club, Amy Tan. Wonderful.

Staggerford and *A Green Journey*, Jon Hassler. A delightful discovery. All his novels are worth reading.

The Sheltering Sky, Paul Bowles. Engendered much lively discussion.

1991

Tending to Virginia, Jill McCorkle. Good in spots.

The Sound and the Fury, William Faulkner. A lot of work, but a big hit.

The Sign of Four, Arthur Conan Doyle, and *The Silence in Hanover Close*, Anne Perry. This was meant to be a compare and contrast of Victorian mysteries, but unless members know something of the mystery genre, discussion is difficult.

Leaving Brooklyn, Lynne Sharon Schwartz. Very good.

To the Lighthouse, Virginia Woolf. Several members described this as the best book they'd ever read.

The Heart Is a Lonely Hunter, Carson McCullers. A popular choice.

The Mill on the Floss, George Eliot. A good read for long winter evenings.

Affliction, Russell Banks. An interesting exploration of character and violence.

A Message to the Planet, Iris Murdoch. Group found it overwhelming.

1992

Philadelphia Fire, John Edgar Wideman. Some hated it; some loved it.

Naked Lunch, William Burroughs. General consensus was "brilliant, but disgusting."

American Appetites, Joyce Carol Oates. An interesting study of violence.

The Golden Notebook, Doris Lessing. Reaction depended on age and perspective.

A Passage to India, E. M. Forster. Big hit.

East Is East, T. Coraghessan Boyle. A very funny sendup of, among other things, writers' colonies.

Typical American, Gish Jen. A popular choice.

The Wanderers, Richard Price. Well written, but some people had difficulty with the depictions of violence.

The Magus, John Fowles. Fake profound.

Slouching Toward Bethlehem, Joan Didion, and *Without Feathers*, Woody Allen. Didion holds up a little better than Allen.

War and Peace, Leo Tolstoy. What a sense of accomplishment!

Ordinary Love and Good Will, Jane Smiley. Two wonderfully crafted novellas that occasioned much discussion.

SELECTIVE BOOK LIST

Marian G. Schott
Mt. Kisco, New York

1984–1985

So Big, Edna Ferber
Germinal, Émile Zola
Heartbreak House, George Bernard Shaw
Winter's Tales, Isak Dinesen
The Color Purple, Alice Walker
Matter of Time, Jessamyn West
Peter the Great, Robert K. Massie
One Writer's Beginnings, Eudora Welty

1988–1989

Portrait of an Artist: A Biography of Georgia O'Keeffe,
   Laurie Lisle
A Summons to Memphis, Peter Taylor
Tongues of Flame, Mary Ward Brown
Mayor of Casterbridge, Thomas Hardy

Beloved, Toni Morrison
Love in the Time of Cholera, Gabriel García Marquez
The Bonfire of the Vanities, Tom Wolfe
Carpenter's Gothic, William Gaddis

1991–1992

Pillars of the Earth, Ken Follett
Madame Bovary, Gustave Flaubert
Mrs. Bridge and *Mr. Bridge*, Evan S. Connell
Cymbeline, Shakespeare
I Know Why the Caged Bird Sings, Maya Angelou
Crampton Hodnet, Barbara Pym
You Just Don't Understand, Deborah Tannen
To Know a Woman, Amos Oz

1992–1993

Angle of Repose, Wallace Stegner
The Betrothed, Alessandro Manzoni
The Crucible, Arthur Miller
Object Lessons, Anna Quindlen
Jazz, Toni Morrison
Women of Deh Koh, Erika Friedl
Remains of the Day, Kazuo Ishiguro
Nobel Prize Author Selection, Nadine Gordimer

SELECTIVE BOOK LIST FROM THE LITERATURE CLUB OF HASTINGS-ON-HUDSON

Mary Scioscia, Hastings-on-Hudson, New York

One of the most enjoyable and rewarding activities in my life is attending my reading club meetings. Officially, it is the Literature Club of Hastings-on-Hudson, and it is more than eighty-four years old, with the first meeting taking place in 1905 or 1906 (the records are unclear). We meet every other Wednesday at a member's house. In March we choose the theme for the next year, and we each choose an author whose writing represents the theme. We then study the author thoroughly so that we can present a program where we describe the author's work, something about his or her life, and the critical reception the writing received. Below is a highly selective list of themes our club has studied during a given year and some of the works or writers we've focused on while exploring those themes.

1976–1977: *English Novelists of the Twentieth Century*

Arnold Bennett
J. R. R. Tolkien

E. M. Forster
Margaret Drabble
Angus Wilson
Virginia Woolf
Dorothy M. Richardson
John Braine
George Orwell
Rumer Godden
H. G. Wells
Joseph Conrad
Somerset Maugham

1977–1978: *The Short Story in the Twentieth Century*

Katherine Anne Porter
Conrad Aiken
Sean O'Faolain
Peter Taylor
John Updike
Eudora Welty
John O'Hara
William Trevor
Paul Gallico
Joyce Carol Oates
Alberto Moravia
Isaac Bashevis Singer

1978–1979: *Letters*

Sylvia Plath
Jane Carlyle
Mozart
Stephen Leacock
Horace Walpole
Mark Twain
Edmund Wilson

Bernard Berenson
E. B. White
Margaret Mead
Anne Morrow Lindbergh
Alexander Solzhenitsyn
Edna St. Vincent Millay
Anne Sexton

1980–1981: *Women Writers*

Colette
Whodunits by women
Rebecca West
Mary Renault
Willa Cather
Isak Dinesen
Sarah Orne Jewett
Nadine Gordimer
Lady Antonia Fraser
Mary Soames
Katherine Anne Porter
Selma Lagerlaff
Katherine Mansfield
Phyllis McGinley
Eudora Welty

1981–1982: *Authors Tell of Their Travels*

Graham Greene in Africa and Mexico
The Alhambra as Writers Have Seen It
Europeans' Travels in America
Lawrence Durrell
Boswell's Tour of the Hebrides
King Lake—Travels from the East
The Peripatetic Robert Louis Stevenson
Henry James's Italian Travels
Thoreau in Maine

Charles Dickens in America
Travels in Greece
Flaubert in Egypt and the East
Travels in Russia
Mark Twain the Traveler

1989–1990: *Children's Literature and Poetry*

Mother Goose
Katerine Paterson
William Blake
George MacDonald
Longfellow
Lewis Carroll
Rumer Godden
Robert Louis Stevenson
Robert Browning
Arabian Nights
C. S. Lewis—*The Chronicles of Narnia*
Elizabeth George Speare
Edward Lear
Rudyard Kipling

HIGHLY SELECTIVE
BOOK LIST OF
THE MODERN
LITERATURE CLUB

Ellen Shipley and Kim Harington
Fayetteville, Arkansas

1926–1930

A Doll's House, Henrik Ibsen
Arms and the Man, George Bernard Shaw
King's Henchmen, Edna St. Vincent Millay
Magic Mountain, Thomas Mann

1931–1940

Cakes and Ale, Somerset Maugham
Herman Melville, Lewis Mumford
Alien Corn, Sidney Howard
Ulysses, James Joyce
A House Divided, Pearl Buck
The Last Puritan, George Santayana
Absalom, Absalom!, William Faulkner

1941–1950

Joseph in Egypt, Thomas Mann

Let the People Sing, J. B. Priestly
Swann's Way, Marcel Proust
Hollywood: The Movie Colony and the Movies, Leo Rosten
Black Boy, Richard Wright
The Trial, Franz Kafka

1951–1960

World Within World, Stephen Spender
The True Believer, Eric Hoffer
Lady into Woman, Vera Britten
The Last of the Wine, Mary Renault
One Hundred Poems from the Chinese, Kenneth Rexroth
The Exile, Albert Camus

1961–1970

The Feminine Mystique, Betty Friedan
Short Friday, Isaac Bashevis Singer
The Proud Tower, Barbara Tuchman
Tally's Corner, Elliot Liebow
North Toward Home, Willie Morris
Maximum Feasible Misunderstanding,
    Daniel Patrick Moynihan
Darwin and the Beagle, Alan Moorehead

1971–1980

I Know Why the Caged Bird Sings, Maya Angelou
Losing Battles, Eudora Welty
On Death and Dying, Elizabeth Kubler-Ross
Pentimento, Lillian Hellman
Emperor of China, Jonathan Spence
Architecture of the Arkansas Ozarks: A Novel,
    Donald Harington
Of Woman Born, Adrienne Rich

Good as Gold, Joseph Heller (note: members usually enjoy their books, as they choose them, but this brought a truly scathing review)

1981–1992

Sophie's Choice, William Styron
Burger's Daughter, Nadine Gordimer
Innocent Blood, P. D. James
Growing Up, Russell Baker
Waterland, Graham Swift
The Letters of Evelyn Waugh, Mark Amory, ed.
White Noise, Don DeLillo
So Long, See You Tomorrow, William Maxwell
What's Bred in the Bone, Robertson Davies
Tales of Arturo Vivante, Vivante
Rabbit at Rest, John Updike
White People, Allan Gurganus
The Generation of 2000, Contemporary American Poets, William Heyen, ed.
Crash Diet, Jill McCorkle
Palace Walk, Naguib Mahfouz

DISCUSSION BOOKS: DEERFIELD PUBLIC LIBRARY

Martha Sloan
Deerfield, Illinois

What Am I Doing Here, Bruce Chatwin. A skillful writer with wonderful observations made while traveling in remote and unusual places. It is, however, difficult to discuss travel books.

What's Bred in the Bone, Robertson Davies. A complex book, perfect for discussion, as are Davies's other novels.

Inconvenient Women, Dominick Dunne. Too superficial for a good discussion.

Soviet Women: Walking the Tightrope, Francine du Plessix Gray. This book about the various roles of Russian women lends itself to interesting discussion.

Family Pictures, Sue Miller. A little too much dysfunctional family for some members, but nevertheless good for discussion.

The Power and the Glory, Graham Greene. A great choice for any group.

Not Without My Daughter, Betty Mahmoody. The members liked this current story, which led to some interesting comments.

Remains of the Day, Kazuo Ishiguro. A seemingly simple story, this intense character study leads to a good discussion.

Staggerford, Jon Hassler. A good choice for a contemporary look at small-town life in rural Minnesota.

The Sun Also Rises, Ernest Hemingway. People have strong opinions about Hemingway, thus this book was an excellent selection.

There Are No Children Here, Alex Kotlowitz. This book's subject matter lends itself to too many personal opinions.

Palace Walk, Naguib Mahfouz. This prize-winning novelist's trilogy of Egyptian life is an interesting look at a different culture and tradition.

Father Melancholy's Daughter, Gail Godwin. Interesting characters make this contemporary novel a good selection.

Wild Swans, Jung Chang. This autobiography of a Chinese woman's life over the past forty years gives a fascinating history of events in China.

Lady Chatterley's Lover, D. H. Lawrence. Lots of fun to rediscover.

Emma, Jane Austen. Perfect.

Son of the Morning Star, Evan Connell. Too detailed and bloody.

The Bean Trees, Barbara Kingsolver. Universally loved.

The Music Room, Dennis McFarland. Interesting discussion.

The Man Who Walked Through Time, Colin Fletcher. It's difficult to discuss travel books this slight.

BOOK
LIST

Liz Stahl
Longmeadow, Massachusetts

1976–1977

The Hunchback of Notre Dame, Victor Hugo
Miss Lonelyhearts, Nathaniel West
Keys of the Kingdom, A. J. Cronin
Three Stories, Yukio Mishima
I, Robot, Isaac Asimov
Humboldt's Gift, Saul Bellow
The Book of Job, Bible, and *J.B.*, Archibald MacLeish
Ordinary People, Judith Guest

1977–1978

Bridge on the Drina, Ivo Andric
The Turn of the Screw, Henry James
The Bridge of San Luis Rey, Thornton Wilder
Anna Karenina, Leo Tolstoy
Cheri and *The Last of Cheri*, Colette

The Short Reign of Pippin IV, John Steinbeck
Women in the Shadows, Ann Cornelisen
Rashomon, Ryunosuke Akutagawa
Pentimento, Lillian Hellman

1978–1979

The Children's Hour, Lillian Hellman
John Cheever short stories
The Painted Bird, Jerzy Kosinski
The Painted Word, Tom Wolfe
Everything That Rises Must Converge, Flannery O'Connor
Stone Angel, Margaret Laurence
The Red and the Black, Stendahl
Truman Capote short stories
My Mother, Myself, Nancy Friday
A Room of One's Own, Virginia Woolf

1979–1980

The Brothers Karamazov, Fyodor Dostoevsky
Winter of Our Discontent, John Steinbeck
Stranger in a Strange Land, Robert Heinlein
Diaries of Anais Nin, Anais Nin
King Lear, Shakespeare
Letters for the Earth, Mark Twain
Shosha, Isaac Bashevis Singer
Three Plays by Sean O'Casey
Candide, Voltaire

1980–1981

Swann's Way, Marcel Proust
Zorba, Nikos Kazantzakis
As I Lay Dying, William Faulkner
Snow Country, Yasunari Kawabata
Two Plays by George Bernard Shaw
The Moon and Sixpence, Somerset Maugham

The Third Wave, Alvin Toffler
Sons and Lovers, D. H. Lawrence

1981–1982

The Covenant, James Michener
Heart of Darkness and *The Secret Sharer*, Joseph Conrad
Out of Africa, Isak Dinesen
Song of Solomon, Toni Morrison
Lelia (The Life of George Sand), Andre Maurois
Lathe of Heaven, Ursula K. LeGuin
Pere Goriot, Honoré de Balzac
The Culture of Narcissism, Christopher Lash
Reinventing Womanhood, Carolyn Heilbrun

1982–1983

The Second Stage, Betty Freidan
Riddley Walker, Russell Hoban
Winesburg, Ohio, Sherwood Anderson
Spring Moon, Betty Bao Lord
A Portrait of the Artist as a Young Man, James Joyce
The Overcoat and Other Short Stories, Nikolai Gogol
Far from the Madding Crowd, Thomas Hardy
Christ Stopped at Eboli, Carlo Levi
A Passage to India, E. M. Forster

1983–1984

Mrs. Dalloway, Virginia Woolf
Buddenbrooks, Thomas Mann
The Color Purple, Alice Walker
Cry, the Beloved Country, Alan Paton
Fifth Business, Robertson Davies
Interpretation of Dreams (abridged), Sigmund Freud
Jorge Luis Borges short stories
Berlin Stories, Christopher Isherwood

1984–1985

Sister Carrie, Theodore Dreiser
Memento Mori, Muriel Spark
The Jesus Incident, Frank Herbert and Bill Ransom
The Women of Brewster Place, Gloria Naylor
Disturbing the Universe, Freeman J. Dyson
The Philosopher's Pupil, Iris Murdoch
Ultima Thule, Henry Handel Richardson
Japanese Inn, Oliver Statler
Under the Volcano, Malcolm Lowry

1985–1986

Hard Times, Charles Dickens
Earthly Powers, Anthony Burgess
The American, Henry James
Kinds of Love, May Sarton
Heart of the Matter, Graham Greene
Pride and Prejudice, Jane Austen
Zen and the Art of Motorcycle Maintenance, Robert Pirsig
A Woman of the Pharisees, Francois Mauriac
My Antonia, Willa Cather

1986–1987

The Aquarian Conspiracy, Marilyn Ferguson
The Wave, Evelyn Scott
Lives of a Cell, Lewis Thomas
The Book of Laughter and Forgetting, Milan Kundera
Selected Short Stories, Alexander Pushkin
Ironweed, William Kennedy
Searching for Caleb, Anne Tyler
The Beans of Egypt, Maine, Carolyn Chute
The Good Mother, Sue Miller

1987–1988

Jane Eyre, Charlotte Brontë
Wide Sargasso Sea, Jean Rhys
The Leopard, Giuseppe di Lampedusa
Vanity Fair, William Makepeace Thackeray
The Handmaid's Tale, Margaret Atwood
Collected Short Stories, Gabriel García Marquez
Disturbances in the Field, Lynne Sharon Schwartz
Among Friends, Letty Cottin Pogrebin
Memoirs of Hadrian, Marguerite Yourcenar
The Old Gringo, Carlos Fuentes

1988–1989

Prince of Tides, Pat Conroy
Dead Souls, Nikolai Gogol
Dubliners, James Joyce
Heat and Dust, Ruth Prawer Jhabvala
House of the Seven Gables, Nathaniel Hawthorne
The Bonfire of the Vanities, Tom Wolfe
The House of the Spirits, Isabel Allende
Beloved, Toni Morrison
In a Different Voice, Carol Gilligan

1989–1990

House of Mirth, Edith Wharton
Frankenstein, Mary Shelley
The Joy Luck Club, Amy Tan
Crossing to Safety, Wallace Stegner
Wind, Sand, and Stars, Antoine de Saint-Exupery
Sister Age, M. F. K. Fisher
White Hotel, D. M. Thomas
Love in the Time of Cholera, Gabriel García Marquez
Family Sayings, Natalia Ginzburg

1990–1991

Dr. Jekyll and Mr. Hyde, Robert Louis Stevenson
Mary Reilly, Valerie Martin
Japanese Mind, Robert Christopher
Remains of the Day, Kazuo Ishiguro
Utz, Bruce Chatwin
Death in Venice, Thomas Mann
Time Will Darken It, William Maxwell
Pioneer Women, Joanna Stratton
Solomon Gursky Was Here, Mordecai Richler
Two Part Invention, Madeleine L'Engle

1991–1992

From Beirut to Jerusalem, Thomas Friedman
Wuthering Heights, Emily Brontë
Treasure of the Sierra Madre, B. Traven
Lucy, Jamaica Kincaid
Bone People, Keri Hulme
Devils of Loudon, Aldous Huxley
Madame Bovary, Gustave Flaubert

1992–1993

Possession, A. S. Byatt
Spartina, John Casey
Composing a Life, Mary Catherine Bateson
Morte d'Urban, J. F. Powers
Daughter of Earth, Agnes Smedley
Waterland, Graham Swift
Christ Stopped at Eboli, Carlo Levi
The Mill on the Floss, George Eliot
To Know a Woman, Amos Oz

THE SISTERHOOD
BOOK LIST

Mary E. Toole
Chicago, Illinois

Breaking Bread, Bell Hooks and Cornell West
Family and *The Matter Is Life*, J. California Cooper
Middle Passage and *Faith and the Good Thing*, Charles Johnson
Invented Lives, Mary Helen Washington
The Brass Bed and *Mad at Miles*, Pearl Cleage
Waiting to Exhale, Terry McMillan
Memory of Kin, Mary Helen Washington
Disappearing Acts, Terry McMillan
Quicksand and Passing, Nella Larsen
Every Goodbye Ain't Gone, Itaberi Njeri
There Is Confusion, Jessie Redman Fauset
Breaking Ice, Terry McMillan
Balm in Gilead, Sara Lawrence Lightfoot
Lemon Swamp and Other Places, Mamie and Karen Fields
The Temple of My Familiar, Alice Walker
I Shall Not Be Moved, Maya Angelou

Possessing the Secret of Joy, Alice Walker
Kindred, Octavia Butler
The Women of Brewster Place, Gloria Naylor
The Endangered Black Family, Nathan and Julia Hare
The Bluest Eye, Toni Morrison
The Big Mama Stories, Shay Youngblood
Crisis in Black Sexual Politics, Nathan Hare
A Dialogue, James Baldwin and Nikki Giovanni
Black Eyed Susans, Mary Helen Washington
Living by the Word, Alice Walker
Earthquakes and Sunrise Missions, Haki Madhubuti
Linden Hills, Gloria Naylor
Some Soul to Keep, J. California Cooper
Women, Race, and Class, Angela Davis
Mama, Terry McMillan
The Blacker the Berry, Wallace Thurman
Praisesong for the Widow, Paule Marshall
Intimate Strangers, Lillian Rubin
Beloved and *Tar Baby*, Toni Morrison
Garvey, Lumumba, Malcolm, Shawna Maglangbayan
Their Eyes Were Watching God, Zora Neale Hurston
The Color Purple, Alice Walker
Homemade Love, J. California Cooper
The Chosen Place, The Timeless People, Paule Marshall
Wild Seed, Octavia Butler
The Street, Ann Petry
Miss Muriel and Other Stories, Ann Petry
Sturdy Black Bridges, Bell, Park, Guy, and Sheftal, eds.
In Search of Our Mother's Garden, Alice Walker
Baby of the Family, Tina McElroy Ansa
Betsey Brown, Ntozake Shange
Gorilla, My Love, Toni Cade Bambara
Corregidora and *Eva's Man*, Gayl Jones
Black Men: Obsolete, Single, Dangerous, Haki Madhubuti
Daughters, Paule Marshall

Drylongso, John Langston Guealtney
The Isis Papers, Dr. Francis Cress Welsing
Reena and Other Stories, Paule Marshall
Click, John Williams
Song of Solomon, Toni Morrison
Brown Girl, Brownstone, Paule Marshall
The Bride Price, Buchi Emecheta
Migrations of the Heart, Marita Golden
Sula, Toni Morrison
A Piece of Mind, J. California Cooper

BEST DISCUSSION BOOK LIST

Susanna Tull
Toronto, Ontario, Canada

The Awakening, Kate Chopin. Nineteenth-century feminist novel.

Crossing to Safety, Wallace Stegner. A great story about friendship, priorities, loyalty, and the stages of life. All of Stegner's books prompt lively discussions.

Ellen Foster, Kaye Gibbons. Triumph of the human spirit, told through the voice of a young, southern girl who endures terrible conditions. Very brief, very powerful.

Remains of the Day, Kazuo Ishiguro. Bittersweet reflections of an English butler. Wonderful prose.

A Summons to Memphis, Peter Taylor. Grown children seek revenge for perceived wrongs done to them by their father by interfering in his attempts to find happiness in his old age. Ultimately about forgiveness and forgetting.

The All of It, Jeanette Haign. Irish story of incest, secrets, morality, and Catholicism. A surprising book.

A Yellow Raft in Blue Water, Michael Dorris. Three generations of a Native American family reconcile their journeys to womanhood.

The Education of Little Tree, Forrest Carter. A real tearjerker about an orphaned boy who lives with his Native American grandparents. Beautiful story of Indian lore and values.

Kristin Lavransdatter, Sigrid Undset. Nobel Prize–winning trilogy about a woman's life in Norway in the Middle Ages.

Moon Tiger, Penelope Lively. A dying woman tells her version of her life and relationships, which is not at all that which was perceived by others.

100 NOVELS AND SHORT STORIES TO READ AND DISCUSS

Susan P. Willens
Washington, D.C.

Nineteenth-Century Fiction

Pride and Prejudice, Jane Austen
Oliver Twist, Charles Dickens
Wives and Daughters, Elizabeth Gaskell
Madame Bovary, Gustave Flaubert
Middlemarch, George Eliot
Fathers and Sons, Ivan Turgenev
The Ambassadors, Henry James

Fantasy, Experiment, and Love

Tristram Shandy, Laurence Sterne
Wuthering Heights, Emily Brontë
Swann's Way, Marcel Proust
Lady Chatterley's Lover, D. H. Lawrence
Mrs. Dalloway, Virginia Woolf
Ulysses, James Joyce

The Sound and the Fury, William Faulkner
The Trial, Franz Kafka

American Short Stories

Daisy Miller and *The Turn of the Screw*, Henry James
"Young Goodman Brown," "Rappaccini's Daughter," and
   "The Birthmark," Nathaniel Hawthorne
The Magic Barrel, Bernard Malamud
Whatever Rises Must Converge, Flannery O'Connor
The Man That Corrupted Hadleyburg, Mark Twain
"The Bear" and "Spotted Horses," William Faulkner
"A Sentimental Education," Joyce Carol Oates
Seize the Day, Saul Bellow

Innocence and Experience

Vanity Fair, William Makepeace Thackeray
The Age of Innocence, Edith Wharton
The Odyssey, Homer
Don Quixote, Cervantes
Lolita, Vladimir Nabokov
In Love and Trouble, Alice Walker, with *Tell Me a Riddle*,
   Tillie Olsen
The Way of All Flesh, Samuel Butler

Finding Oneself

Tom Jones, Henry Fielding
Losing Battles, Eudora Welty
Notes from Underground, Fyodor Dostoevsky
Invisible Man, Ralph Ellison
"The Big Two-Hearted River," "The Snows of Kilimanjaro,"
   "A Clean Well-Lighted Place," "A Way You'll Never Be,"
   selected stories, Ernest Hemingway
Germinal, Émile Zola
McTeague, Frank Norris

Wonderland, Joyce Carol Oates
Great Expectations, Charles Dickens

Naturalism in America

U.S.A., John Dos Passos
The Red Badge of Courage, Stephen Crane
Studs Lonigan, especially *Young Lonigan*, James T. Farrell
The Awakening, Kate Chopin
All the King's Men, Robert Penn Warren
The Dollmaker, Harriet Arnow
A Death in the Family, James Agee
The Book of Daniel, E. L. Doctorow
Pale Fire, Vladimir Nabokov

Justice and Injustice

Antigone, Sophocles
Crime and Punishment, Fyodor Dostoevsky
1984, George Orwell
Amerika, Franz Kafka
The Lover, A. B. Yehoshua
As I Lay Dying, William Faulkner
Jane Eyre, Charlotte Brontë
King Lear, William Shakespeare
Emma, Jane Austen

Societies and Individuals

War and Peace, Leo Tolstoy
The Death of Ivan Ilych, Leo Tolstoy
Things Fall Apart, Chinua Achebe
House of Mirth, Edith Wharton
Sister Carrie, Theodore Dreiser
Heart of Darkness, Joseph Conrad
Frankenstein, Mary Shelley
One Hundred Years of Solitude, Gabriel García Marquez

Outdoors

Housekeeping, Marilynne Robinson
Moby-Dick, Herman Melville
My Antonia, Willa Cather
Robinson Crusoe, Daniel Defoe
Sons and Lovers, D. H. Lawrence
Thousand Cranes, Yasunari Kawabata
The Call of the Wild and "To Build a Fire," Jack London
To the Lighthouse, Virginia Woolf

Interior Truth

Portrait of a Lady, Henry James
The Good Soldier, Ford Madox Ford
The Women of Brewster Place, Gloria Naylor
Krapp's Last Tape with *Molloy*, Samuel Beckett
The Color Purple, Alice Walker
Persuasion, Jane Austen
Gimpel the Fool, Isaac Bashevis Singer
The Adventures of Huckleberry Finn, Mark Twain

Social Injustice

Bleak House, Charles Dickens
The Joke, Milan Kundera
Badenheim 1939, Aharon Apelfeldt
Out of Africa, Isak Dinesen
The Tin Drum, Gunter Grass
Henry IV, Shakespeare
The Stranger, Albert Camus
Hamlet, Shakespeare

Spiritual Quests Around the World

The Book of Job, Bible, and *J.B.*, Archibald MacLeish
The Palm-Wine Drinkard, Amos Tutuola
Barrabas, Par Lagerkvist

A Fanatic Heart, selected stories, Edna O'Brien
Light in August, William Faulkner
The Makioka Sisters, Junichiro Tanizaki
Life and Times of Michael K., J. M. Coetzee
The Master and Margarita, Mikhail Bulgakov

BOOK
LIST

Kathy Willhoite
Chicago, Illinois

1987

Notes from Underground, Fyodor Dostoevsky
Wise Blood, Flannery O'Connor
Lysistrata and *The Clouds*, Aristophanes
Persuasion, Jane Austen
The Unbearable Lightness of Being, Milan Kundera
Death in Venice, Thomas Mann
The Plague, Albert Camus
A Chronicle of a Death Foretold, Gabriel García Marquez

1988

Silas Marner, George Eliot
The Age of Innocence, Edith Wharton
Pale Fire, Vladimir Nabokov
My Antonia, Willa Cather
The Counterfeiters, Andre Gide

Other Voices, Other Rooms, Truman Capote
Song of Solomon, Toni Morrison
Absalom, Absalom!, William Faulkner
Dubliners, James Joyce
Mrs. Dalloway, Virginia Woolf
Main Street, Sinclair Lewis

1989

Things Fall Apart, Chinua Achebe
The Collector, John Fowles
Catcher in the Rye, J. D. Salinger
Madame Bovary, Gustave Flaubert
The Adventures of Huckleberry Finn, Mark Twain
Sometimes a Great Notion, Ken Kesey
A Confederacy of Dunces, John Kennedy Toole
Alice in Wonderland and *Through the Looking-Glass*,
   Lewis Carroll
The Glass Key, Dashiell Hammett
Lucky Jim, Kingsley Amis
"A Christmas Memory," Truman Capote, and
   "A Child's Christmas in Wales," Dylan Thomas

1990

The Red and the Black, Stendahl
Frankenstein, Mary Shelley
The Awakening, Kate Chopin
Tender Is the Night, F. Scott Fitzgerald
Burger's Daughter, Nadine Gordimer
The Man with a Golden Arm, Nelson Algren
The Joy Luck Club, Amy Tan
Mourning Becomes Electra, Eugene O'Neill
Gulliver's Travels, Jonathan Swift
The Clown, Heinrich Böll
A Fan's Notes, Frederick Exley
Christmas Stories

1991

The Castle, Franz Kafka
The Pickwick Papers, Charles Dickens
Poetry, a varied collection, selected by members
The Loved One, Evelyn Waugh
Zen and the Art of Motorcycle Maintenance, Robert Pirsig
Angle of Repose, Wallace Stegner
A Hero of Our Time, Mikhail Lermontov
Christmas Stories

1992

Howards End, E. M. Forster
The Lincoln-Douglas Debates, selections
Childhood's End, Arthur C. Clarke
Poetry, a varied collection, selected by members
Their Eyes Were Watching God, Zora Neale Hurston
The Comedians, Graham Greene
The Good Soldier, Ford Madox Ford
Nostromo, Joseph Conrad
Delta Wedding, Eudora Welty
Grapes of Wrath, John Steinbeck

HIGHLY SELECTIVE BOOK LIST

Paula Zurowski
Berkeley, California

1975

The Little Disturbances of Man, Grace Paley
Gaudy Night, Dorothy Sayers
A Mingled Yarn, Beulah Parker, M.D.
When She Was Good, Philip Roth
The Dollmaker, Harriet Arnow
Good Morning Midnight, Jean Rhys
The French Lieutenant's Woman, John Fowles
The Bell Jar, Sylvia Plath
Save Me the Waltz, Zelda Fitzgerald
A Very Easy Death, Simone de Beauvoir

1976

The Death of the Heart, Elizabeth Bowen
Men's Liberation, Jack Nichols
Between Myth and Morning, Elizabeth Janeway

The Mandarins, Simone de Beauvoir
Tell Me a Riddle, Tillie Olsen
Looking for Mr. Goodbar, Judith Rossner
A Garden of Earthly Delights, Joyce Carol Oates
The Prime of Miss Jean Brodie, Muriel Spark
The Story of O, Pauline Reage
The Odd Woman, Gail Godwin

1977

The Love Object, Edna O'Brien
Crazy Salad, Nora Ephron
"The Yellow Wallpaper," Charlotte Perkins Gilman
Last Flight, Amelia Earhart
Flowering Judas, Katherine Anne Porter
Birds of America, Mary McCarthy
A Gift from the Sea, Anne Morrow Lindbergh
Passages, Gail Sheehy
Scoundrel Time, Lillian Hellman
The Woman Warrior, Maxine Hong Kingston

1978

Changing, Liv Ullman
Sense and Sensibility, Jane Austen
Lady Oracle, Margaret Atwood
Lovers and Tyrants, Francine du Plessix Gray
Gemini and poetry, Nikki Giovanni
Ethan Frome, Edith Wharton
The Ballad of the Sad Cafe, Carson McCullers
Through the Flower, Judy Chicago
Slouching Towards Bethlehem, Joan Didion
A Member of the Wedding, Carson McCullers

1979

And I Alone Survived, Lauren Elder

An Unsuitable Job for a Woman, P. D. James
Bruno's Dream, Iris Murdoch
The Grab, Maria Katzenbach
Justine, Lawrence Durrell
Nuclear Madness, Dr. Helen Caldecott
The Mermaid and the Minotaur, Dorothy Dinnerstein
The Makioka Sisters, Junichiro Tanizaki
The Well of Loneliness, Radclyffe Hall
Pilgrim at Tinker Creek, Annie Dillard

1980

Maurice, E. M. Forster
Attachments, Judith Rossner
The Women's Room, Marilyn French
Diet for a Small Planet, Frances Moore Lappe
Imaginary Friends, Alison Lurie
Chamber Music, Doris Grumbach
O Pioneers!, Willa Cather
Blackberry Winter, Margaret Mead
The Left Hand of Darkness, Ursula K. LeGuin
Blood Tie, Mary Lee Settle

1981

Herland, Charlotte Perkins Gilman
Mrs. Munck, Ella Leffland
Lolita, Vladimir Nabokov
Meridian, Alice Walker
The Ballad and the Source, Rosamond Lehmann
Marry Me, John Updike
The Wife of Martin Guerre, Janet Lewis
Alice in Wonderland, Lewis Carroll
Billy Budd, Herman Melville
Summer, Edith Wharton

1982

A Few Green Leaves, Barbara Pym
The Doctor's Wife, Sawako Ariyoshi
The Odd Women, George Gissing
Great Expectations, Charles Dickens
The Facts of Life, Maureen Howard
Innocent Blood, P. D. James
Rich Rewards, Alice Adams
The Moonstone, Wilkie Collins
The Second Coming, Walker Percy
St. Joan, George Bernard Shaw

1983

Clea, Lawrence Durrell
Spring Moon, Betty Bao Lord
Dusty Answer, Rosamond Lehmann
Mary Barton, Elizabeth Gaskell
Soul of a New Machine, Tracy Kidder
Face to Face, Ved Mehta
Death Kit, Susan Sontag
The Promise, Chaim Potok
Esmond in India, Ruth Prawer Jhabvala
Daughters and Rebels, Jessica Mitford

1984

Honourable Estate, Vera Brittain
Life Sentences, Elizabeth Hailey
Our Nig, Harriet Wilson
Catch a Fire: Biography of Bob Marley, Timothy White
The Bostonians, Henry James
Tirra Lirra by the River, Jessica Anderson
Sister Age, M. F. K. Fisher
During the Reign of the Queen of Persia, Joan Chase
Moll Flanders, Daniel Defoe

Dona Flor and Her Two Husbands, Jorge Amado

1985

Excellent Women, Barbara Pym
The Name of the Rose, Umberto Eco
Terms of Endearment, Larry McMurtry
The Little Drummer Girl, John LeCarre
We Have Always Lived in the Castle, Shirley Jackson
Ironweed, William Kennedy
In My Mother's House, Kim Chernin
A Tale of Two Cities, Charles Dickens
Stones for Ibarra, Harriet Doerr
Dreams of Sleep, Josephine Humphreys

1986

Nicholas and Alexandra, Robert Massie
A Room with a View, E. M. Forster
If on a Winter's Night a Traveler, Italo Calvino
One Writer's Beginnings, Eudora Welty
A Russian Journal, Andrea Lee
The Sea Change, Elizabeth Jane Howard
Resurrection, Leo Tolstoy
Men and Angels, Mary Gordon
The Catcher in the Rye, J. D. Salinger
Hard Choices, Kathleen Gerson

1987

Nuns and Soldiers, Iris Murdoch
The Iliad, Homer
Long Day's Journey into Night, Eugene O'Neill
The Myth of Women's Masochism, Paula Caplan
Miss Peabody's Inheritance, Elizabeth Jolley
Ceremony, Leslie Marmon Silko
The Shadow Knows, Diane Johnson
Foreign Affairs, Alison Lurie

Aunt Dan and Lemon, Wallace Shawn
The Mind-Body Problem, Rebecca Goldstein

1988

You Can't Go Home Again, Thomas Wolfe
The Monkey's Wrench, Primo Levi
The Fountain Overflows, Rebecca West
Monkeys, Susan Minot
Daughter of Earth, Agnes Smedley
Ideas and the Novel, Mary McCarthy
Iacocca, Lee Iacocca
The Spectator Bird, Wallace Stegner
Golden Days, Carolyn See
Medea, Euripides

1989

Survival in Auschwitz, Primo Levi
And the Band Played On, Randy Shilts
The Old Gringo, Carlos Fuentes
Anywhere but Here, Mona Simpson
Oedipus Rex, Sophocles
The Mask of Apollo, Mary Renault
Mrs. Caliban, Rachel Ingalls
Nelly's Version, Eva Figes
Picture Bride, Yoshiko Uchida
Loving Kindness, Anna Roiphe

1990

A Dinner to Die For, Susan Dunlap
On the Black Hill, Bruce Chatwin
Paris Trout, Peter Dexter
The Great Divide, Studs Terkel
The Blooding, Joseph Wambaugh
The Life and Loves of a She-Devil, Fay Weldon
In Country, Bobbie Ann Mason

Geek Love, Katherine Dunn
Nothing to Declare, Mary Morris
Family Sayings, Natalia Ginzburg

1991

Disappearing Acts, Terry McMillan
Enemies, A Love Story, Isaac Bashevis Singer
Among School Children, Tracy Kidder
You Just Don't Understand, Deborah Tannen
A Gathering of Old Men, Ernest Gaines
This Boy's Life, Tobias Wolff
Rumors of Peace, Ella Leffland
Sexing the Cherry, Jeanette Winterson
Light in August, William Faulkner
The Education of Little Tree, Forrest Carter

1992

Possession, A. S. Byatt
A Sport of Nature, Nadine Gordimer
The Things They Carried, Tim O'Brien
Hocus Pocus, Kurt Vonnegut
The Crown of Columbus, Louise Erdrich and Michael Dorris
Hedda Gabler and *A Doll's House*, Henrik Ibsen
East Is East, T. Coraghessan Boyle
Patrimony, Philip Roth
Mariette in Ecstasy, Ron Hansen
How to Make an American Quilt, Whitney Otto

An Invitation to
Book Group Members

If you are a member of a book group and would like to be considered as a contributor to future editions of *The Book Group Book*, please send your name, address, telephone number, and a brief description of your group (no more than 250 words, please) to:

Editor, *The Book Group Book*
Chicago Review Press
814 N. Franklin Street
Chicago IL   60610